PRACTICAL
SOCIAL WORK

BASW

Editorial Advisory Board:
Robert Adams, Terry Bamford, Charles Barker, Lena Dominelli,
Malcolm Payne, Michael Preston-Shoot, Daphne Statham and
Jane Tunstill

Social work is at an important stage in its development. All
professions must be responsive to changing social and economic
conditions if they are to meet the needs of those they serve. This
series focuses on sound practice and the specific contribution which
social workers can make to the well-being of our society in the
1990s.

The British Association of Social Workers has always been conscious of its role in setting guidelines for practice and in seeking to
raise professional standards. The conception of the Practical Social
Work series arose from a survey of BASW members to discover
where they, the practitioners in social work, felt there was the most
need for new literature. The response was overwhelming and
enthusiastic, and the result is a carefully planned, coherent series of
books. The emphasis is firmly on practice, set in a theoretical
framework. The books will inform, stimulate and promote discussion, thus adding to the further development of skills and high
professional standards. All the authors are practitioners and teach-
ers of social work, representing a wide variety of experience.

JO CAMPLING

PRACTICAL SOCIAL WORK
Series Editor: Jo Campling
BASW

Robert Adams *Self-Help, Social Work and Empowerment*

David Anderson *Social Work and Mental Handicap*

Sarah Banks *Ethics and Values in Social Work*

James G. Barber *Beyond Casework*

James G. Barber *Social Work with Addictions*

Peter Beresford and Suzy Croft *Citizen Involvement: A Practical Guide for Change*

Suzy Braye and Michael Preston-Shoot *Practising Social Work Law*

Robert Brown, Stanley Bute and Peter Ford *Social Workers at Risk*

Alan Butler and Colin Pritchard *Social Work and Mental Illness*

Crescy Cannan, Lynne Berry and Karen Lyons *Social Work and Europe*

Roger Clough *Residential Work*

David M. Cooper and David Ball *Social Work and Child Abuse*

Veronica Coulshed *Management in Social Work*

Veronica Coulshed *Social Work Practice: An Introduction (2nd edn)*

Paul Daniel and John Wheeler *Social Work and Local Politics*

Peter R. Day *Sociology in Social Work Practice*

Lena Dominelli *Anti-Racist Social Work: A Challenge for White Practitioners and Educators*

Celia Doyle *Working with Abused Children*

Angela Everitt, Pauline Hardiker, Jane Littlewood and Audrey Mullender *Applied Research for Better Practice*

Kathy Ford and Alan Jones *Student Supervision*

David Francis and Paul Henderson *Working with Rural Communities*

Michael D. A. Freeman *Children, their Families and the Law*

Alison Froggatt *Family Work with Elderly People*

Danya Glaser and Stephen Frosh *Child Sexual Abuse (2nd edn)*

Bryan Glastonbury *Computers in Social Work*

Gill Gorell Barnes *Working with Families*

Cordelia Grimwood and Ruth Popplestone *Women, Management and Care*

Jalna Hanmer and Daphne Statham *Women and Social Work: Towards a Woman-Centred Practice*

Tony Jeffs and Mark Smith (eds) *Youth Work*

Michael Kerfoot and Alan Butler *Problems of Childhood and Adolescence*

Joyce Lishman *Communication in Social Work*

Carol Lupton and Terry Gillespie (eds) *Working with Violence*

Mary Marshall *Social Work with Old People (2nd edn)*

Paula Nicolson and Rowan Bayne *Applied Psychology for Social Workers (2nd edn)*

Kieran O'Hagan *Crisis Intervention in Social Services*

Michael Oliver *Social Work with Disabled People*

Joan Orme and Bryan Glastonbury *Care Management: Tasks and Workloads*

Malcolm Payne *Social Care in the Community*

Malcolm Payne *Working in Teams*

John Pitts *Working with Young Offenders*

Michael Preston-Shoot *Effective Groupwork*

Peter Raynor, David Smith and Maurice Vanstone *Effective Probation Practice*

Carole R. Smith *Adoption and Fostering: Why and How*

Carole R. Smith *Social Work with the Dying and Bereaved*

Carole R. Smith, Marty T. Lane and Terry Walsh *Child Care and the Courts*

David Smith *Criminology for Social Work*

Gill Stewart and John Stewart *Social Work and Housing*

Christine Stones *Focus on Families*

Neil Thompson *Anti-Discriminatory Practice* ·

Neil Thompson, Michael Murphy and Steve Stradling *Dealing with Stress*

Derek Tilbury *Working with Mental Illness*

Alan Twelvetrees *Community Work (2nd edn)*

Hilary Walker and Bill Beaumount (eds) *Working with Offenders*

Family Work with Elderly People

Alison Froggatt

MACMILLAN

First published 1990 by
THE MACMILLAN PRESS LTD
Houndmills, Basingstoke, Hampshire RG21 2XS
and London
Companies and representatives
throughout the world

ISBN 0–333–44655–0 hardcover
ISBN 0–333–44656–9 paperback

A catalogue record for this book is available
from the British Library.

Printed in Hong Kong

11	10	9	8	7	6	5	4	3
03	02	01	00	99	98	97	96	95

Series Standing Order

If you would like to receive future titles in this series as they are published, you can
make use of our standing order facility. To place a standing order please contact your
bookseller or, in case of difficulty, write to us at the address below with your name
and address and the name of the series. Please state with which title you wish to
begin your standing order. (If you live outside the United Kingdom we may not have
the rights for your area, in which case we will forward your order to the publisher
concerned.)

Customer Services Department, Macmillan Distribution Ltd
Houndmills, Basingstoke, Hampshire RG21 2XS, England

Contents

Preface

It has proved difficult to disentangle the complicated interrelationships of the ideas and issues in writing about vulnerable elderly people and their families to help social workers develop this area of practice. I have been trying to combine two aspects. As a social worker and social work teacher I am very aware of the reality and value of family network care for those old people who become dependent in some way. This understanding is underpinned by a wish to find ways to practice which offer alternatives and additions to family care where required, so that such care becomes less onerous and exploitative of family feelings of warmth and affection. This would benefit both carers and cared for. First, some of these issues will be discussed. Then, by describing a range of methods I hope social workers will be encouraged to value the challenge of richness and complexity in family work with elderly people. The reality of the complex problems that social workers face is demonstrated by some case studies. All names are fictionalised and circumstances have been slightly altered to preserve confidentiality.

The first chapter discusses the significance of society's emphasis on the family, and the diversity of later life families. This leads on to an exploration of intergenerational relationships in later life which are not well understood. These have to be seen in relation to the developmental stages in any family's life-cycle. The concept of family networks and family systems is developed, drawing on social systems theory. A psychosocial approach to the experience of old age for any individual, to which is added some awareness of health factors, enhances professional understanding of the situation. The personal experience will also be affected by the ageism, racism and sexism in society as a whole. The experience of growing older in a multiracial and possibly alien environment is particularly important and not yet well understood. After this broad introduction the subsequent chapters will explore methods of social work practice using case examples.

Social work with later life families is usually practised from a social service department. The background to social service provision is explored in Chapter 2, with emphasis also placed on interdisciplinary co-operation. The process of assessment is discussed, leading to social care planning with the client and family.

In the third chapter the statutory basis of social work is acknowledged, and consideration given to aspects of work which require particular skill and sensitivity from the social worker. Issues of loss, becoming old in a strange country, sexuality, mental impairment, alcoholism, and elder abuse are discussed.

The fourth chapter focuses on ways to communicate and develop individual work, using a variety of skills in service provision, or counselling around a particular issue. In particular, crisis intervention and task centred work are described. Some aspects of psychotherapy also provide insights which are helpful.

The fifth chapter is about working with families and carers, the family system as a whole. This is in many ways the heart of the book, for one has to understand the complexity of caring relationships to contribute effectively as a social worker. Drawing on family therapy, ways to set up family meetings are discussed.

The crisis that may arise from the admission of an elderly family member to residential care is the subject of the sixth chapter. Clarification of the role of the social worker in this social system and ways of working with residents and their families in that setting are suggested.

By contrast, the seventh chapter turns outwards towards neighbourhood work and community developments, in the interests of maintaining family links and networks in a multiracial society.

The final chapter draws these themes together. Family work with vulnerable elderly people and their relatives demonstrates the highest skills of professional social work practice. The political and societal aspects of service provision within existing community care policies provide added pressure for social workers in an ageist society. Social workers who can recognise the personal demands of social work with elderly people have a deeper understanding to contribute in all aspects of their work. There is a need to campaign for more respect for old people and their families, those who do the caring, and recognition for workers at all levels in welfare services who assist them.

Acknowledgements

Many have shared their ideas and practical help. Among social workers, students and colleagues I particularly want to thank Elaine Berry, Janet Burrows, Stuart Cameron, Lynn Chambers, Stephen Collins, Faith Gibson, Jeff Hearn, Tom Kitwood, Tiu Kujando, Barbara McCabe, Mohammed Mossadeq, Susan Parker, Margaret Rees, Claire Stevens, Jill Stevens, Martin Truelove, and Prim Wright.

The Advisory Panel on Ageing of BASW, the Centre for Policy on Ageing, and friends met through the British Society of Gerontology are all part of a network to whom I am grateful. As editor, Jo Campling has been a steady source of reassurance and advice. David Froggatt has given invaluable support in so many ways.

ALISON FROGGATT

1

People in Later Life

Introduction

The aim of this book is to foster good social work practice with elderly people and their families. It is addressed primarily to social workers and social work aides but may be useful to those working in residential and day care settings and those supporting social care in the community. The first chapter sets out to clarify our understanding of vulnerable elderly people in relation to their families. It is recognised that old people and their families are disadvantaged in the amount of care and attention paid to them by social workers as most social work time is spent on children and young families. There are compelling societal priorities and pressures to carry out policies of child protection. However, some of the disinterest of social workers reflects the inherent ageism in our society. In general old people who are becoming vulnerable in some way, are left to carry on coping with the assistance of family, friends, or neighbours, and most receive minimal help from outside welfare agencies. For example, only 34 per cent of the most severely disabled elderly people receive a home help (Victor, 1983, p. 303). Government policy extols the virtue and normality of family care (DHSS, 1981) but does not underpin the policy with sufficient resources.

In economic and statistical terms people whom we define as old are usually taken to be men and women over 65. Ninety-three per cent of people in this age group live in their own homes or with relatives (OPCS, 1984; Wheeler, 1986, p. 219). Relatively few are in hospitals or residential accommodation. Those at home are usually part of a family network or social support network. As a person's independence gradually gives way to dependence in one or more areas of daily life, it is generally accepted that the family will increase support and assistance. This picture incorporates a good many complexities in reality. Social workers may need to take time to clarify the nature of the social and family network, and the reciprocal exchanges within it. Reciprocity is common in family life. The exchange of goods and services throughout the life-span has been explored (Finch, 1987c; Harper, 1987) emphasising how parents help young adults financially and with child care, in return for practical and financial help in old age.

In considering some elderly peoples' transition from independence, first to interdependency, and possibly to dependency prior to death, there are a number of points to bear in mind which are outlined here, to be explored more fully later in the chapter.

Retirement

The position of retired people ensures a degree of economic dependency for many, and poverty in a good many cases, which accentuates all other difficulties.

Poverty

Sixty-six per cent of pensioners live on the margins of poverty, which increases with age (Walker, 1986, p. 185). A broad distinction must be observed between young-old people aged 65–74, old-old people aged 75–84, and very old people aged 85 and upwards. Within these age bands there are very wide variations in capability. The age span 65–100 is such that some families may have two generations in retirement, with young-old people as carers of very old parents. One sibling may care for another, or there may be a three-pension household.

Independence

Individuals have a right to some independence, and areas of choice in their style of living whatever the degree of their eventual infirmity. The structured dependency of old age feeds a culture that regards passivity as an inherent aspect of growing old (Phillipson and Walker, 1986). This should be resisted by social workers interested in developing good practice. Vulnerable elderly people and their carers are equal actors in the drama of their caring relationships. The carers' needs must be taken on board as well.

Diversity

Diversity and complexity in living arrangements and family patterns in later life compel analysis of the nature and significance of the family, family networks and family system. The character of inter-generational relationships reflects the earlier history and experience of each member of that family and their shared life.

Multiracial society

The experience of any person incorporates biological and psycho-social aspects of life, including some experience of the inherent racism, sexism, and ageism in society. Thus for some people, living in an alien multiracial society may present particular problems which need appropriately sensitive solutions (Norman, 1985).

Gender

Society makes a different response to old men and to old women, sometimes resulting in the greater denigration of older women; this takes some combating on a personal and a professional level (Sontag, 1978; Macdonald and Rich, 1984). Men are more likely than women to receive services if they are in a caring role (Charlesworth *et al.*, 1984).

Social services

Complicated tasks face social service departments in trying to meet the claims for service made on them and to offer constructive assistance within statutory responsibilities and resource constraints.

Action

There is a need to take a proactive stance to develop social work with elderly people and their families, as the welfare state contracts, and a mixed economy of welfare emerges. A patchwork of care may well be required that is drawn from private and voluntary as well as formal and informal sources. A campaigning approach is needed to seek better resources and develop greater understanding.

Definition of terms

Before exploring the complexity of social work with old people it is necessary to clarify some of the terms used. This is not purely an academic exercise. It is helpful for understanding the situation of elderly people and possible intervention.

The family   A useful definition is: 'a kinship network spanning three or more generations and involving relatives who do not necessarily live in the same house' (Graham, 1984, p. 17).

Family network   This involves neighbours, friends and other informal carers, as well as formal carers such as home help or the peripatetic warden, involved on a daily basis with an individual old person. The term 'social support network' also carries the same meaning but is descriptive of a more loosely structured set of connections with fewer family members.

Family system   The process of day-to-day interaction within the old person's family network. This necessarily affects the principal carer, the main relative and the formal carer who is the key worker as well as the individual or partnership in question.

Principal carer   This is the person carrying most responsibility for day-to-day care. It might be spouse, sibling, son or daughter, friend, warden, home help.

Vulnerable old person   This term will be used to distinguish the small number of very frail old people from the majority of competent independent elderly people over 65.

Social worker   This term will be used for those undertaking a professional social work role, whether operating in field work, residential or day care.

Informal care   A euphemism for care given by friends, family and neighbours without payment (Green, 1988). The term carer or family carer will be used to denote those doing unpaid family care.

Formal Care   Professional workers paid to intervene by a statutory organisation, such as district nurse, home help, warden, social worker.

Dependant   Some government publications talk about informal carers and the dependants they care for (Green, 1988). The word dependant will not be used in this way as a noun.

Other terms will be defined in context where appropriate.

While this book is primarily about the various methods social workers can develop in work with elderly clients and their families it is necessary to first explore a number of major theoretical issues which bear on practice as follows:

1   later life families and their relationships;
2   social systems theory;
3   experiencing vulnerability in old age;
4   social services and social work with families.

Later life families and their relationships

To begin to explore the nature of family life in our society we have to recognise that personal and political elements are interwoven in all family life.

1. To understand the *personal* element it helps to recognise the significance of primary attachment figures. All carers have had parenting of some sort, leaving a residue of affection, resentment, ambivalence, and other complex emotions in relation to those parental or proxy parental figures. This holds true regardless of our current status, as single, married, co-habiting, divorced, widowed adults with or without children of our own. These personal responses to discussions of parental figures should be recognised by social workers in preparation for working in this area. There is otherwise a possibility of transferring feelings relating to personal circumstances to those of clients or consumers or residents, and their families. Secondly, the feelings about parental figures are strong; this is an emotionally highly charged area to work in, where each person's experience will be unique; family rules and prohibitions handed down through the generations hold sway. Thirdly, this whole area

has been undisclosed, little discussed, acknowledged, and shared. The complexities of later family life are just beginning to be recognised with studies of intergenerational caring relationships (Nissel and Bonnerjea, 1982; Abrams and Marsden, 1987; Ungerson, 1987).

2. In understanding the *political* dimension of issues involving later life families, it helps to look behind government policy in Britain, which since the 1980s has re-emphasised the care of old people in and by their families (DHSS, 1981). There is a determination to defend the family as an essential part of the social organisation for social care, viewed in both the private and the public sphere. As part of this ideology the family is seen as not only the appropriate place to rear and nurture children, but also the fitting place to care for dependent and distressed family members who are disabled or very elderly. Many writers recognise that family care is care provided predominantly by women (Nissel and Bonnerjea, 1982; Finch and Groves, 1983; Ungerson, 1987; Dalley, 1988). The Equal Opportunities Commission (1980) found three times as many women as men were carers but a later study of informal care discovered a larger proportion of male carers (Green, 1988).

The whole emphasis on family care has developed building on a somewhat distorted view of past patterns of family life. It ignores the fact that in the late nineteenth-century individualism was a driving force and yet paradoxically collective care was also valued, hence the building of large institutions and hospitals (Dalley, 1988). We need to understand these two aspects of the personal and the political. The strong personal ties of affection and responsibility which bind families are intrinsically valuable, meeting basic needs for security and identity, but can at times be claustrophobic and destructive. These ties bear hardest on those who tend to accept moral responsibility for caring roles. The needs of individuals would appear to conflict with the emphasis on the family. Both fit within a view of society in which men are heads of families. Women, children and dependent adults are all subsumed within a man's family, and their capacities for individuality and self-expression are of secondary importance, seen from this perspective. This at least often seems to be the majority view in the indigenous culture of our society. In a somewhat similar way in some other cultures family honour and obligations are of paramount importance, and the needs of individuals are secondary. Social workers will need to think through their own views on the value and purpose of the family.

Defining the family

In favouring family care for elderly people in the 1980s (DHSS, 1981) government policy had a pattern of family life in mind. As Rossiter and Wicks (1982, p. 63) explained: 'It includes all or many of the following characteristics: an elderly relative living with or near her family: a stable nuclear family and an able-bodied woman at home supported financially by her husband at work'. They go on to point out that the typical family of (working) father and (house-wife) mother make up 15 per cent of households (Rimmer, 1981, p. 62). This so-called norm is in fact atypical of the majority of young families, failing to take account of widow(er)hood, divorce, remarriage, and of single parents. Similarly, in later life families there are diverse patterns. Companionate relationships, hetero-sexual, gay, or lesbian, may be as long lasting as marriage.

If we accept that more of the caring is done by women the second problematic issue for family care of elderly people is the number of women who expect to be employed outside the home. The majority of women expect to be in employment. In 1983, 68 per cent of non-married women aged 16–59 were in employment, and 61 per cent of married women (OPCS, 1984). Thus a carer's role may be fitted in on top of employment and domestic responsibilities.

Thirdly, the characteristics of later life families have changed over time. The increase in the number of very old people over 85 is up from 1.03 per cent of the population in 1981 to an estimated 1.9 per cent in 2001 (Phillipson and Walker, 1986, p. 5). On average, women live six years longer than men, and men tend to marry younger women. Some women and men never marry, or are no longer married, being widowed or divorced; 80 per cent of women over 75 and 39 per cent of men at the same age are on their own. So we develop a general picture of the most vulnerable elderly people being very old women living alone. There is a tendency for men and women to move in with siblings or younger relatives in extreme old age (Peace, 1986, p. 63). Most people of middle age are or have been married; divorce affects all age groups. Some elderly people have been through a divorce leaving a residue of ambivalent feelings and some social isolation (Hunt, 1978, Table 12:8:1).

Divorce and remarriage of the middle generation will affect the care of elderly people, for how many ex-in-laws are likely to be cared for by ex-sons and daughters-in-law? Each remarriage may bring attendant relatives to be cared for. A decision might have to be made about the number of elderly people for which it is possible to take responsibility in any one family. These decisions may well also be affected by geographical mobility both for employment and retirement. There is evidence that men are taking early retirement or using redundancy to take on a caring role (Green, 1988). The effect of unemployment, especially on men, as potential family carers is not yet much researched. It may be hard to move away from traditional gender roles at a time of unemployment.

Looking ahead to the early twenty-first century, the smaller size of nuclear families in the late twentieth century makes it evident that there will be fewer relatives about to share family care although it is likely that many fewer people will be childless (Rossiter and Wicks, 1982,p. 66). Relationships with siblings, perhaps especially for those who are childless, remain important in old age (Wenger, 1984).

These factors indicate that the families of vulnerable elderly people are not easy to define. Above all the setting from within which family care might be provided is not a static one. The relationships in any family will have their own characteristics, reflecting the personalities and histories of the family members, to be considered in the next section.

Understanding the older family

There are several aspects of life in the older family to disentangle, in order to begin to understand the family system, and the family network of any elderly person or couple referred for social work help. These are:

1   Developmental stages: the current stage in the life-cycle of the elderly person, and the current stage which their 'children' as middle-aged, or young-old adults have reached.
2   The psychological response each member of the family has to his/her stage in the life-cycle.

3   The nature of the interaction between generations.
4   The specific pattern of behaviour of a particular family – the
    family system.
5   The wider family network surrounding the elderly person.

Developmental stages in the second half of life

Developmental psychologists (Gould, 1978; Erikson, 1965, 1978)
have responded to the growing number of older families with an
interest in understanding the stages of life that occur from forty
onwards. These might be described as:

1   the 'empty nest' as children leave home;
2   the mid-life review or mid-life crisis, male and female 35–55;
3   pre-retirement preparation 55–64;
4   retirement and young-old age 65–74;
5   old age 75–84;
6   very old age 85 onwards;
7   death as a certain event of unpredictable timing.

One of the markers of the second half of the life cycle is the
recognition that life has an inevitable end. It is not possible to
describe all these stages fully here but others have done so elsewhere (Fogarty, 1985; Neugarten, 1968).

It should be noted that these stages are to a considerable extent
socially and economically determined. The status of retired people
as non-contributory dependents is intensified by government policy
(Phillipson, 1982). Gender and race also affect the position and
status of older people.

Psychological responses to life-cycle changes

Individual women and men are bound to vary enormously in the
way they experience the psychological and material changes in the
later part of the life-cycle. Most changes will be accompanied
by both loss and gain: the loss of children leaving home, the gain in
extra leisure and space for example. How a person perceives
changes may be affected by how it is perceived by other members of
the family and society. The needs of other generations may also

affect behaviour. A newly retired couple who want a holiday may put pressure on a very old relative not to complain of feeling ill. A woman seeking employment in her forties may not want to recognise the deterioration of her mother-in-law's memory.

Interaction between generations

In older families this may pose some problems, not least about 'who's in charge'. In the nuclear family with small children it is clear that parents normally are in charge. They hand over responsibility to teenage, growing up and growing away, young people, who should gradually feel they are in charge of their own lives, and eventually become fully independent.

For many years a companionate relationship may exist between two generations of adults in a family, each leading an independent existence. However, a trigger event or crisis may become important as that system of mutual independence becomes altered into one of interdependence. The experience of becoming an adult child taking filial responsibility for an elderly parent or another aged relative, has been documented in American literature (Blenkner, 1965). To describe this stage as interdependence takes away the stigma of attempting to parent a parent, assuming a role reversal. To do that denies the reality that a person once a parent is always a parent, in some sense, to their children. If the reciprocal roles and activities which occur in a family in the mutual interdependency phase can be sorted out, it enhances the status and well-being of each side, so that we see a grandmother who mends while her daughter does the washing, an old person baby-sits while the young neighbour does shopping.

The fact of taking charge or taking responsibility for a vulnerable elderly relative requires considerable moral courage which tends to fall to women (Graham, 1983; Ungerson, 1987). It is a complex experience with dimensions of intermixed love and affection, duty and obligation. The moral courage required on the part of the elderly person to recognise what is happening and not resist should also be saluted.

The family system

As part of understanding any family system the organisation of the pattern of behaviour over time is very important (Gorell Barnes, 1984, p. 7). Much of what we do in daily life is done by habit, which may be passed down from one generation to another. So the nature of the domestic organisation, or disorganisation, the roles adopted, the division of tasks within a family, the ways of communicating, and expressing feelings verbally and non-verbally, must all be taken into account in exploring the significance of interaction. This material forms the basis of planning for purposeful social work activity.

The family network

The family network includes all those involved with a vulnerable elderly person on a very regular basis. For some old people who live alone the 'family system' may include neighbours, home help, district nurse, or relative visiting weekly. Each of these may make a daily or weekly contribution which interweave to form a family network. The complexities of this network must be understood, and will be explained more fully in Chapter 7 together with suggestions on ways social workers may help to sustain or develop such a network. Those in the network may be so closely involved with the old person as to become part of the family system (see Chapter 5).

Social systems theory can further our understanding of these last two points.

Social systems theory

In the 1970s theorists in the United States of America (Pincus and Minahan, 1973; Goldstein, 1977) and in the United Kingdom (Specht and Vickery, 1979) developed a social systems theory drawing on the general systems theory widely used in biological science. This helps by showing that social systems can be viewed as consisting of:

1 an individual with his/her intrapersonal system of living incorporating psychological and sociological factors;
2 the dyad, a system of two interrelated people with their interpersonal system;
3 larger interpersonal systems, the small group, or family with their interconnections;

4   the larger social system, the large community institution, organisation, or even neighbourhood (Specht and Vickery, 1979, p. 5).

Secondly, each system is able to respond to internal and external pressures, and indeed must do so. The aim is to achieve a kind of steady state, which preserves the system as a whole by some adaptive mechanism, such as a change of role, structure, or exclusion of one member. The social worker whose aim is to effect change in response to some cry for help, will try to ensure that the change occurs in such a way that it is manageable for the system as a whole.

The unitary model of Specht and Vickery has been further developed to explore social support networks (Whittaker and Garbarino, 1983). Greene (1986) suggested that social work with old people needs to incorporate this dimension. Her study describing a family network for each client is the overriding theoretical framework being adopted in this book. It is particularly appropriate for social work practice with vulnerable elderly people. A social worker is usually involved because a person has ceased to be fully independent in some aspect of daily living. Then the neighbours and family who are relied on to share some daily task become more evidently part of the social system, or family system of that elderly person.

By taking a broader view of the family network than that provided solely by kin, one can explore the network of relationships which are significant to the client. Pincus (1981, p. 56) described the value of this kind of network:

> Where an old person is still to be seen at the centre of a web of relationships that extend down the generations and through the individual members to the community beyond it can be quite startling how the pleasure derived from life remains undiminished despite quite severe physical and material handicaps.

Within the family itself, each member contributes as part of the system, being in some way a member from birth through to death, so that the system has a long history. On a day-to-day basis there may be influence in the interaction between one member and another, which will be demonstrated by verbal or non-verbal feedback. The contributions of family members who live at a distance should not be under-estimated. What happens to one member affects others, practically and emotionally. There may well be a typical family response to a crisis, a pattern of behaviour which is the norm for that system.

Greene (1986) explored the family system approach writing for gerontological social workers in America. Given that intervention usually follows a crisis, she encouraged a focus on:

1   finding out how functional changes in the old person affect the whole family system. These changes may be shown by a failure in health, or morale, or by bereavement;
2   the way the family is structured and organised. This will affect the way family members respond to the change in capacity of the elderly family member, including how the family system can incorporate these changes;
3   the developmental stage of any family must be taken into account since the family will be adapting to changing pressures from younger as well as older members. Are the younger generation all living independently, or is the middle generation under pressure from both sides? Some families might include five generations.

Sometimes different events contribute to vulnerability as people become very elderly. The reaction of each individual will be personal and it is hard to find out how this is experienced.

Vulnerability in old age

Among the key points to remember in developing good practice with vulnerable elderly people are:

1   the uniqueness of individual experience;
2   the necessity of taking a biological and psychosocial approach;
3   the importance of the social world with its opportunity for reciprocity;
4   private and public attitudes to vulnerability in old age in a multiracial society;
5   the recognition of the resources available to any individual.

Unique individuals

You cannot divorce a person from her/his history. Very old people talking about themselves find having an aged body a matter of disbelief (Hemmings, 1985; Froggatt, 1985). The person inside so often retains a strong feeling of individuality and continuity, as demonstrated by the poem 'The Crabbit Old Woman' (Carver and Liddiard, 1978). In this, the old woman in hospital chides the nurses on the ward to 'see me' who was once young and vigorous, with children. Thus emphasis on reminiscence sensitively developed (Coleman, 1986) and oral history are all part of a recognition that by listening to the memories and past experience of an elderly person we are validating the unique worth of that individual, the contribution made to society.

The bio-psychosocial approach

In encouraging social workers to take this approach to understanding and assessing a vulnerable elderly person, one is recognising the significance of functional capacity and coping ability. Health and degrees of disability are affected by many other factors which are psychological and sociological in origin. Being ill results from a combination of pressures. Indeed the very definition of illness is related to a decision-making process which involves responding to symptoms by taking action to seek advice. Illness behaviour in old age has been found to be not substantially different from that of younger people (Victor, 1987, p. 268).

It is true that with increased years the incidence of multiple pathology increases. An elderly person may become frail because of the combination of illnesses or disabilities. The main areas of difficulty have been described as instability, incontinence, immobility, and intellectual impairment (Isaacs, 1980). These are easy to remember and are said to occur together in combinations which are difficult to treat, and require an interdisciplinary team of helpers. One in eight of the population over 65 is severely disabled, and twice that number moderately disabled (Phillipson and Walker, 1986, p. 6). These impairments may or may not lead to functional disability, resulting in a handicap. To consider the impact one must explore details of everyday life and discuss these with the elderly person in the context of the family network. Psychological resources must also be taken into account to see if the basic requirements for daily life can be met. One person with immobilising arthritis might continue to cope alone sustained by a network of friends and family. A more socially isolated person might become depressed and forgetful, and not be able to cope.

The social world

As well as the family network we must acknowledge the social world, the network of reciprocal roles and relationships, past and present. The wider extended family of distant kin and friends may include some who have died, but who are present in memory. Other roles and relationships are ongoing, or still to come, such as becoming a grandparent or great-grandparent. The extent of the social world depends on proximity and geographical mobility, but the use of the telephone, letters, cassettes and videos can bridge distance.

Most old people are contented with the amount of contact with their family members (Victor, 1987, p. 222). Wenger (1984, p. 91) found that more than half the childless old people in her study of rural Wales saw a relative, a sibling, niece, nephew or cousin at least once a week, though in inner city London there were more isolated old people (Sinclair *et al.*, 1984).

To supplement relatives, close friends are important. Jerrome (1982) has explored the significance of a confidante for older women in maintaining life satisfaction, even if that person is only seen once a year. Murphy (1983) recognised the value of friendship in warding off depression. Some of the depression may be a response to bereavement. Wenger (1984) identified that the death of a sibling or friends may be harder to get over than the death of a spouse, perhaps because the longevity of the relationship goes back to earliest years.

Most women have greater life expectancy than men. Women of 60 can expect to live to 80, men of the same age to 75 (Victor, 1987, p. 109). It is possible that women will experience more occasions of loss and loneliness in extreme old age. We should not forget that the experience of ageing may well be different for men and women. Some women (internalising sexism) may feel even more devalued without a man with whom to be identified. This is balanced by a growing recognition of the potential that older women have to be proactive in their own lives (Hemmings, 1985). It is hoped that this will gradually lessen the passivity which has been a characteristic response of some women to multiple loss. It has been shown that a number of older women remain 'active initiators' as in earlier life, rather than becoming 'passive responders', even when being cared for (Evers, 1983).

The social world will be much affected by race, creed, class, gender, and culture. The expectations of what should be provided, in contrast with what is available, may be painful for some from minority groups.

Attitudes to ageing and to elderly people in a multiracial society

Ageism permeates society at both ends of the life-cycle. Children are denigrated by adults, and as Itzin (1984) has identified this discrimination sows the seeds for later ageism towards very old people. Ageism seems to be partly triggered off by a fear of becoming old and dependent, and so a reluctance to identify or even empathise with the oldest people. Ageism is also structurally determined by policy documents which denigrate the growing number of very old people as a non-productive burden by such terms as *The Rising Tide* (Health Advisory Service, 1983).

The experience of being an old person, a senior citizen, is imposed from outside, as for example people find when they first queue up for a retirement bus pass: 'The general expectation [is] that old people should be incompetent' (Victor, 1987, p. 265). Norman (1987b) is aware that ageism affects social workers and social service delivery, in the low expectation of change that might be possible.

In the multiracial, multicultural society which the United Kingdom has become, there are adjustments to be made on all sides. Both institutional and personal racism may be experienced by elderly people and their families.

As part of society, elderly clients and their carers may be contributors to a racist or anti-racist society by what is said or done. Some ethnic minority elders may find the continuing experience of hostility and racial abuse which they experience very hard to bear. As one Afro-caribbean elder said in an old peoples' club: 'It is not only the climate that is cold in England' (Grant, 1988). Institutional racism may become apparent in difficulties in gaining access to health and social services. Other indigenous elderly people with set ideas may find it hard to come to terms with living in a multiracial community, and being offered care by a member of a minority group. As statutory services continue to implement an equal opportunities policy these matters will need sensitive handling by social services.

Recognition of individual resources

Old age is not a sudden event: those becoming dependent must have anticipated and prepared for this stage in some characteristic way, even if by denial. It is fruitful to recognise the responsibility people have for their own lives, and the material circumstances in which those lives have been lived, in considering the resources with which a person enters the last stages of life. These resources will include primarily the family and/or social network, with which this book is concerned.

Secondly, there are resources of skill and wisdom. Those whose educational opportunities have been greater in earlier life may be in a stronger position to take advantage of facilities in the community, as will those with a strong local network. The resources of continuing health, sight, hearing and memory should also be acknowledged. Characteristics such as a strongly independent spirit, a generosity of personality, and an appreciative warmth are assets.

Financial resources must often be explored with elderly people, despite the discomfort this may arouse in client and social worker. Those with limited means may need help with welfare entitlement. There are charges for many local authority services, some of which are means tested, including residential care. 55 per cent of old people are owner-occupiers of the homes they live in (Wheeler, 1986, p. 219). The capital value of these may be high. Admission to any form of residential care whether private, voluntary or local authority will probably require a careful review of assets, savings and income.

If an old person is admitted to local authority residential care while still having a house to sell, some of the value of the property when sold may be claimed back by the authority in retrospective residential charges. It is important to find out the regulations in the local authority concerned. The value of the property will be taken into account if a DSS subsidy is required for private or voluntary care.

Apart from housing, financial resources often reflect opportunities in earlier life. Some have a substantial occupational pension, and possible capital accumulation which might allow for the provision of goods and services in a period of dependency.

In inflationary times almost every ageing person experiences some anxiety about how their finances will hold out, leading to severe economies over food, fuel, and replacement of clothing and household goods. The level of the basic retirement pension is such that those who rely on it must either live a frugal existence (Holman, 1986), take part time jobs for as long as possible to make ends meet or claim income support. Poverty is often associated with old age for the longer people live the less the value of their pension or savings, and the greater the expense of providing care in increasing disability (Townsend, 1979; Phillipson and Walker, 1986). As people become more frail there may be increased reluctance to think of applying for income support: 1.1 million people were living below the old supplementary benefit level and the take up rate was 67 per cent (Walker, 1986, p. 185).

Summary

In this chapter some of the important matters relevant to an understanding of family work with elderly people have been discussed. Elderly people are almost always in some sense part of a family with kin-related and social support networks. Any change in the vulnerable elderly person's capacity to cope with daily living should be considered in relation to his/her place in the family network, and the capacity of that network to respond to the change. To that end the development of a wider understanding of intergenerational relationships has been encouraged. One should also explore the present capacities of the client against the background of the life experience which shaped him/her.

In the next chapter we consider how to translate these insights into action, starting with an exploration of the social services agency base for providing services and social work help.

Vulnerable elderly people becoming dependent and disabled in some way, who, with their families, seek assistance, must look to a wide spread of provision under the mixed economy of welfare. Statutory provision by social service departments can meet some needs, but others are increasingly being met by the voluntary and private sector, as well as by friends and relatives, informally and without pay. The concern here is especially with social service provision, and the place of social work within it.

2

Making a Start

This chapter explores the social service base for undertaking social work with elderly clients, and the need to work with other professionals in interdisciplinary co-operation from the beginning of many cases. The process of developing a referral is followed through, showing how assessment leads into a piece of planned social work offering social care, using case studies as examples.

Introduction to social services

Social service provision for old people grew out of the Poor Law, and welfare departments, with the 1948 National Assistance Act (Part iii) laying a responsibility on local authorities to provide residential care for certain categories of old people. The function of the family as the principle and necessary carer was recognised by policy makers from at least 1948 onwards. The 1968 Seebohm Report recommended: 'an adequate overall service for the old to which anyone in need can be referred with the certain knowledge that appropriate action will be taken where necessary' (Seebohm, 1968).

This report emphasised: 'the care which the family gives its older members is of prime importance. Nothing is quite an adequate substitute . . . social service departments should make every effort to support and assist the family which is caring for an older member'.

Thus support for families who are helping to care for an elderly frail relative was built into the activities planned for social service departments from the beginning. The provision of a social work service for elderly people is one of the responsibilities of local authorities as set out in the Local Authorities Social Services Act 1970. There is also a requirement to provide a range of domiciliary support, to provide residential care, and to encourage voluntary and individual initiatives. The extent to which this is not being accomplished reflects the competing pressures on those authorities.

On first referral to the agency an elderly client has to provide evidence of need, by demonstrating some degree of incapacity to warrant receipt of a service. The assessment of need at point of referral will be undertaken by the social worker on duty, or by the Home Help Organiser if a home help is requested. Allocation to the appropriate worker for further services may be undertaken by the team leader, calling on a social work assistant or occupational therapist. A qualified social worker is seldom used in work with vulnerable elderly people in many agencies (Black *et al.*, 1983; Howe, 1986).

The Seebohm Report emphasised family work with elderly people, but the social workers skilled to do this seldom receive the opportunity; many seem willing to accept the inevitability of case loads taken up by high priority child protection. Although it is recognised that a major proportion of referrals to social service departments are about elderly clients (Black *et al.*, 1983), the allocation of referrals concerning elderly people tends to go to untrained social work assistants or students. The dangers of allocation by client group to certain categories of worker was recognised by Buckle who wrote: 'Inherent in the use of certain grades of worker wtih particular client groups is a denial of the emotional and relational problems of those client groups dealt with by social work assistants' (Buckle, 1981, p. 174).

In such circumstances an incomplete service is being offered for social work as a service. This is not to deny the immense amount of valuable warm support and practical help given to old people by social work assistants. To watch an unqualified and inexperienced social work assistant wrestling with the intractable relationships of an elderly client, makes one realise that it is not just the client who is being unjustly treated, in a system of blanket allocation by client group.

The ambivalence about providing services for elderly people was reflected in the report of the Audit Commission (1985) which analysed dependency and service provision without specifically mentioning the field workers who will do much of that work. There was very little sign in this report of constructive planning to use social work skills to support old people and their carers.

The constraint for social workers wanting to do family work with elderly clients is to be allowed the time to do it at all. A way forward indicated in the Wagner Report (1988, p. 3.6) identified a role for a nominated social worker. This builds on the work of the Kent Community Care Project. The key worker or case manager role, identified in the research, uses social work time productively to help maintain a vulnerable person in his/her home, and not using more costly residential care. This requires understanding by manager and social worker alike (Davies and Challis, 1986). The Griffiths report (1988, p. 6.4) recommended regular assessment, with appropriate supporting services arranged through social service authorities.

Interdisciplinary co-operation

In many situations social workers need to work closely with several members of other disciplines or professions in meeting the needs of elderly people and their families. Primary health-care teams, headed by general practitioners, and including district nurses, health visitors and nursing aides are allies of social workers in maintaining a knowledgeable and supportive network of services. Liaison with hospital staff, and the rehabilitation team of physiotherapists, occupational therapists and speech therapists may be useful for some clients (Squires, 1988). Some of these specialists are also community based.

Within the social services department liaison may be involved with the home care service, residential and day care establishments, wardens and sheltered housing to help maintain a client at home. A number of officials in the local authority, housing, environmental health, and professionals in the community could also be involved. The police, fire and ambulance services, religious leaders, and even corner shops and post offices may all be part of the social support network for an elderly client. Information from any of these people may be helpful in completing an assessment and planning future care.

The capacity to co-ordinate work with a variety of professionals, each with a different perspective and set of priorities is one that takes time and skill to develop. It helps to recognise aspects of the training and professional orientation of different workers. Problems may arise in terms of the hierarchy of professionals, in that the medical profession may attempt to adopt a prescriptive role towards a social service department, reluctant to accept the judgement of a different agency on priorities. Exploration of relationships between different sorts of general practitioners and varied types of social workers indicates that stereotyping can be as dangerous in this area of relationships as in any other (Huntingdon, 1981).

A considered effort to develop interdisciplinary co-operation was planned as part of the Dinnington Project (Bayley *et al.*, 1987). This project is useful for the analysis and an example of how to improve interdisciplinary relationships. A regular fortnightly meeting of practitioners from different backgrounds, with a shared task, helped to develop trust over time. First it was necessary for participants to recognise how little they understood of each others' work, and then to begin to formulate ways of working as a team. They had to achieve managerial recognition that accountability to colleagues in the team was important alongside accountability to individual agencies. Multidisciplinary forums have been established to co-ordinate work for vulnerable elderly people in certain areas (Burton and Dempsey, 1988).

This account of interdisciplinary work is necessarily brief. Other examples of ways to liaise in practice will be given as often as possible.

Family work

Family work with elderly people as described in Chapter 1 involves the elderly person, the immediate family members, the family network, and the much wider social support network reaching out into the neighbourhood. The context for social workers comes from the referral of an old person to the agency, an action taken by the individual him/herself, or by a relative, neighbour, or another professional worker. The referral offers the social worker an immediate opportunity to start to practise family work, by setting out the questions which need clarification. The answers to those questions almost always incorporate significant people in the client's family network. The social worker can then decide whom to interview. By drawing in family members one is showing recognition that what happens to the vulnerable old person has an impact on others in the social support system. This sets the framework for doing a bio-psychosocial assessment, using multidisciplinary knowledge from other professionals to piece together the impact of recent events on a particular family network.

This will probably be followed by indirect social work involving social care planning, and direct social work with the client and one or more of the family members, in one of a variety of ways.

Social work in a social services setting

The client

The term 'client' is widely used within social services and social work practice, to refer to those people who come to the attention of the agency as being in need of some assistance or service. It is an ambiguous term, with connotations from legal practice of employing a professional to safeguard one's interests. The power relationship within a social worker/client interaction is not always of that order. There are times when a social worker has to act against the client's wishes, and as a form of protection, in exceptional cases, deprive a person of responsibility for their affairs, or even of their liberty. This statutory framework will be discussed in Chapter 3. Despite this ambiguity, the term 'client' is used in this book to distinguish those who are about to be, or already are in a relationship with the agency through the attention of a social worker.

When the name of a vulnerable elderly person has been passed to a social services department, that person becomes at least temporarily a client. The details of name, address, and brief details of the identified difficulty, entered on the official form, become a referral. The referrals are usually sorted by a team leader, put in order of priority, and allocated to social workers. It is at this point that elderly people often lose out, such is the pressure to give top priority to protective work with small children. Many referrals will be dealt with by the duty officer and never allocated to a social worker.

The referral form is physically passed to the social worker or social work assistant in the allocation process, indicating that it is that person's responsibility to initiate action on behalf of that client. It would be good practice never to accept a referral without the knowledge and consent of the client, but issues of risk and protection with vulnerable elderly people sometimes lead to a decision to override that principle. The passivity of the client at this point is apparent; it is up to the social worker to give back some power, by talking with the client about his/her perceptions of the situation before taking any other action.

Acting on a referral

On receiving a referral a social worker can usefully begin by setting out answers to these questions:

What is the problem?
Why is it a problem?
To whom is it a problem?
Why is it a problem now? (adapted from Marshall, 1988, p. 41)

Thus one starts with an indication that more than one person may be affected by the problem, and that there may have been a crisis or trigger-event leading to a referral for assistance at this point.

The social worker should interview the client first, and obtain permission to contact other people. It requires skill to be allowed to draw in family members or other professionals, to give a multi-disciplinary picture. Sentences such as: 'It would help to have your daughter's opinion.' 'It may be you see things differently.' 'May I contact your doctor to see if she/he can help us?' can help restore the initiative to the client, and if the client says 'No', this can be discussed. It is always possible, and often successful, to return to the subject having given the person a chance to think things through. Once consent is given it is possible to plan further discussions and interviews, or a family meeting.

It is valuable to collect information from the family network, and from involved professionals, as by weighing up and balancing different contributions it is possible to build up a picture of recent events to complete an assessment.

Assessment

The assessment process begins with the initial screening of referrals by the duty officer, taking messages and doing short intake interviews. The team leader does a further assessment before deciding whether a social worker or social work aide should take on the referral. Once allocated it should be a prime task of the particular worker to do a full assessment, in the knowledge that this may need to be repeated, as the health, morale or circumstances of the elderly person at risk can change rapidly with a knock-on effect.

At least an hour should be allowed to conduct an interview with a vulnerable elderly client, in order to begin an assessment. The presenting problem should be recognised, for example, 'Your niece wondered if you would like us to arrange for you to come out for the day once a week?' This might be a referral which presented and was interpreted as specifically for day care.

Alternatively an introductory sentence might be: 'I've come to talk about how you are managing at the moment.' Some broad term such as 'managing' offers scope for the client and the social worker to explore the necessary details of daily life, such as shopping, making meals and snacks, attending to the toilet, dressing, washing, getting about, and loneliness. At the same time as having the conversation, the social worker should be observing behaviour and the surroundings. The differences in behaviour and attitude, such as self-confidence, agitation, apathy, or restlessness should be noted. It helps to ask the client's permission to jot down a few facts. This kind of generalised discussion can at the same time draw in a number of points covering health aspects, daily routine, and the emotional needs for company, and a sense of belonging which if not met can result in depression, anxiety or misery. The 'why now' factor really does need checking out. What recent event has led to a referral at this point? A change of home help, a fall, or a recent bereavement might any of them result in a sense of not being able to cope, and thus to a referral.

It is only by balancing up all the factors, getting the degree of difficulty perceived on all sides, that the whole picture becomes clear. England (1986) emphasised both evaluating a person's ability to cope, and developing an understanding of the meaning of the experience for the individual concerned. Social service departments in general, and social workers in particular have no wish to interfere in peoples' lives unless there are difficulties, of which inability to cope with current circumstances is the most obvious. This raises questions of standards, and here with old people one should listen to their life experience and life style in judging standards. Thus an old person who lives alone surrounded by piles of newspapers and plastic bags full of shopping and old clothes may be quite happily engaged in a long-term sorting out of possessions on a scale that may take years to accomplish. If the bags are full of rotting food, or there is a smell or filth around the place, then more action *may* need to be taken, but the first priority is establishing what the person concerned feels, before asking 'Would it be helpful for someone to come in and give a hand with tidying up?'

The primary health care team may have an understanding of what the old person and the carers are experiencing and should be consulted. It is increasingly recognised that a full medical assessment is helpful if a change of residence is planned, such as admission to a residential home.

As part of an assessment a careful written record should be made identifying needs, wants and feelings, resources and unmet needs. Too often there is a confusion between a service oriented definition of needs rather than a problem-oriented one (Goldberg, 1987, p. 608). Needs are often those aspects of care identified and defined by others: 'He/she needs day care.' But, of course,the client has wants and feelings: 'I want my husband back. I want to live nearer my sister. I feel lonely.'

Needs and wants are often similar, but it is good practice to assume there may be a distinction. The resources in a situation need recording fully too. A broad approach should be taken in this appraisal. The factors to be noted might include such aspects as 'limited mobility', 'a clear mind', or 'a purpose built flat'. This is to keep sight of the positives for so often professionals working with very vulnerable elderly people focus on the pathology and forget what the client may have going for her/him. Finally in matching wants and resources one might be able to identify unmet needs, for which future services might be planned.

In assessing needs a social service worker is doing three things:

1 identifying what would help the individual;
2 seeking to allocate appropriate resources;
3 comparing the needs of one person with another where resources are scarce.

There is often an element of risk attached to unmet needs. A risk arises where there is a potential predictable hazard, and part of the risk equation is deciding on what balance of probability the danger is likely to arise (Brearley, 1982).

CASE STUDY 2.1

A newly blind old woman living alone was referred by her next door neighbour for a place in a residential home. She did not want to go, but lived in an unmodernised house with a coal fire as the main source of heat. The position had been reached where she could not make out the labels on the cans of food she was heating up. She was feeling for the lumps of coal in her fuel store, to bring them in to light the fire in snowy weather. One had to evaluate the fire risk for her and her neighbour, in helping her to come to terms with giving up her independence and moving into residential care as soon as a place became available.

A final element to bear in mind are the concepts of primary secondary and tertiary care (Richards, M., 1987). Is the care required likely to come from mobilising resources in the neighbourhood, through self-help groups, and existing communal facilities, thus requiring primary care? Are there significant areas of difficulty likely to require active involvement of a social worker with an individual or a family as in secondary care? Is the situation so serious that twenty-four hour care must be considered, whether the person is at home or considering going in to a residential home? Tertiary care is the most complex kind of care to provide and get right. It is possible that a mixture of all three levels of care might be indicated to meet the needs of one client. We have to recognise the level of skill required, and especially support those offering twenty-four hour care in whatever setting.

Family members should be interviewed to consider their view of the situation, how they think family interaction patterns are disturbed by recent events, and what might be helpful. Then when all aspects have been explored, as far as time permits, the worker should enter the social care planning phase and decide what services might be offered.

In summary the assessment of a client with his/her family network requires that the social worker, or student, or social work aide does the following:

1. Sees and understands any situation in its complexity, the physical, mental, emotional and social factors interacting, the strengths and weaknesses of the client and principal carers, the

meaning of the situation to them all and the impact on the family network and its way of coping.

2. Balances up the wants and needs, the risks involved in the client doing what she/he wants, and/or doing what the carers want, and/or putting the welfare services at risk by default, but in that order of priority. The capacity to manage risk within available resources usually develops with experience, but takes considerable skill (Crosbie, 1983).
3. Negotiates a package of services and adjustments to daily life which is acceptable to all involved.

Assessment offers the space for individualising the vulnerable elderly client. A sophisticated package of services will be useless unless an underlying empathy has been demonstrated, and trust established by the social worker. We have to somehow recognise and then become free of that overwhelming fear of being engulfed by the demands and powerful feelings in some clients and their families. Good practice involves careful listening, giving recognition, with patience. The social worker should give some realistic idea about what services may be possible. That stage is part of what is involved in social care planning.

Social care planning

After assessing the situation, evaluating the strengths and difficulties of the client within the family network, the social worker moves on to social care planning, which has been defined as follows:

1 Plans designed to solve or alleviate existing problems.
2 Plans which aim to prevent the development of social problems in the future.
3 Plans which aim to create or strengthen resources to respond to those which do arise (Barclay, 1982, p. xv).

The concern here is with the first of these points. The plans to deal with existing problems may range from straightforward co-ordination of arrangements for a person leaving hospital, to a much more complex plan with the social worker in the case manager/key worker role (Davies and Challis, 1986), as will be described.

Case management The Kent Community Care Project envisaged a key worker for particularly frail elderly people in the community. Social workers were given specific help in identifying their function to find ways to keep old people at home who might otherwise have gone into a residential home. Experienced social workers were given a case manager role for a small case load of such elderly people, with the task of keeping them in their own homes on a budget of two-thirds the cost of residential care in a local authority home.

The tasks identified were:

'1   close assessment of client need;
2   choosing among alternative ways of providing care, anticipating what could go wrong and juggling resources in emergencies;
3   providing the necessary degree of psychological understanding to suffuse the care system;
4   being judged successful because of the stability and adequacy of the care provided' (Challis, 1982, p. 57).

It should be noted that the fact that the client is part of a family network is implicit rather than explicit in this plan of action.

Through the development of this research programme, a fuller list of tasks was defined which explained the social care planning process in context. Thus social workers undertaking long term care tasks would:

'a) raise suitable referrals;
b) do a careful and detailed assessment;
c) plan a complete package of care;
d) liaise with other agencies;
e) monitor the situation;
f) provide support and advice to elderly people and their families;
g) develop community resources such as lodgings or neighbourly help' (Challis and Davies, 1985, p. 564).

The tasks of planning and liaising, and monitoring are of particular relevance here.

Planning a complete package of care   This rather ugly term 'package of care' has come into general welfare use to describe what is often a complex solution to a client's need for services. Having identified wants and needs and resources as already defined, the social worker has to negotiate the resources and services available from the statutory sector. This will include using knowledge about the availability of home help, meals on wheels, day care, warden service, respite care and a district nurse if required. Voluntary and private services and clubs may also be of use. These will have to be interwoven to meet the particular needs. To do this it is useful to think through in detail the daily routine of the client, what he/she can manage, and where the gaps are. Breakfast and an evening meal can present problems as well as a midday meal. Who is already available and acceptable and willing to help? Negotiations will be necessary with other agencies as well as the client and carers. How receptive is the client to the help being offered? Having a home help may seem an insult to a very independent person. Going to 'day care' may involve too early a start for someone who has become a night owl while living alone. So the possible services and what each would involve should be talked through with everyone concerned, interweaving the contributions from friends and family with available services into a coherent system of support understood by all.

A significant aspect to consider is the vulnerability of the client to being left alone, and unattended. Can the person be left alone for a week, a day or two hours (Isaacs and Neville, 1976)? The risk of a very old person falling and being left for a long period lying on the floor is a sufficient anxiety to encourage some families to opt for residential care for their elderly family member, when with enough support it might not be necesssary (Challis and Davies, 1985, p. 571). Social care planning might aim for admission to residential care, if the person was sufficiently isolated, anxious and incapacitated to warrant this. Authorities vary in how much residential care is available, and neighbourhoods differ in the amount of private residential homes and the take up of DSS funds to help pay the fees. Yet family and friends may well need help in planning for such an admission; this way the older person does not feel rejected, but is admitted taking a social network of support with them, of people who will visit regularly, and not feel guilty (see Chapter 6). The cost of local authority residential care is so great that much emphasis is put on keeping people in their own homes. The Audit Commission (1985) set out a framework for identifying degrees of dependency, bearing in mind that each person at home saved the state £3000. Making up packages of care can merely increase the burden on those carers, unless they are fully consulted and involved; some of the services need to be geared to support them.

Monitoring services   Once the services have been arranged it is tempting for social workers to withdraw from the situation. However, it is essential to monitor that services are working. There may have been a breakdown in communication; the taxi for day care did not call, the officer in charge was abrupt, the meal unsuitable; these are matters not hard to put right, but unless sorted out quickly, enough to put off an elderly person perhaps reluctant to face a change of routine or the challenge of meeting new people. If the social worker is clear about the level of ongoing responsibility for the situation, wanting feed back about how arrangements worked out, this may well make all the difference to the success of the planning. The question of how long to stay involved is a tricky one involving issues of case load management and consideration of the other pressures and demands. One advantage of allocating a case to a student is he/she may have more time to spend in follow-up. Certainly in many difficult and anxiety-provoking situations carers continue to keep going without much regular social work intervention, provided that those doing the daily caring know that a swift and understanding response will be available if required.

'The effective performance of the core tasks of case management is fundamental to the success of field arrangements for community-based care' (Davies, 1987, p. 170).

Challis and Davies (1985, p. 578) identified two groups of clients particularly suitable for life at home with social care planning as a cost effective answer for social service departments:

(a) the extremely dependent elderly person with mental and physical frailty who receives a considerable degree of informal support.
(b) the relatively isolated elderly person with only a moderate degree of dependency, suffering from a non-psychotic psychiatric disorder.

If such people with planned social care can be kept in their own homes it is worth pressing for flexibility of resources to put in the extra help needed. Although home helps and home care aides now cover a very wide range of duties, payment of voluntary helpers to do specific imaginative tasks outside the range of normal home help duties was not found to diminish the degree of goodwill of informal carers; rather that was enhanced.

The following two cases give examples of the complex nature of family work.

CASE STUDY 2.2 – MR AND MRS FITCH

This elderly couple, Joan Fitch aged 65 and Stanley Fitch aged 67, were referred by a psychogeriatrician after an assessment by the community psychiatric nurse. Mr Fitch a former barman had Korsakoff's disease, a kind of brain failure occurring as a result of alcoholism. His behaviour was becoming unmanageable at home. The background was that Stanley's first wife had died six years previously, and Joan had been her best friend. Joan herself was a widow, and as an ex-nurse she befriended Stanley and began to care for him. She offered to be his housekeeper, but he wanted her to move in with him. The family, her children, were strongly Roman Catholic, and advised against this without marriage, so she married him. This proved a disaster for many reasons. Stanley was a big man whereas his wife was small and thin; he became violent and difficult to live with. His behaviour became anti-social or unpredictable at times. For example, he hid his underpants in the lavatory, and took the cooker apart. Joan found herself increasingly unable to cope, and became a secret sherry drinker. Stanley's family helped initially by taking him out to the pub, but he was worse on his return.

This then was the situation facing the social worker at the time of referral, with Joan at breaking point, and Stanley unaware of the difficulties. She resented having remarried, and his demands, for she had never intended to have a sexual relationship with him. She was not able to sleep at night, finding herself pushed about in bed. Divorce was out of the question, because of her religious convictions. The social worker's approach, having completed her assessment, was to seek some immediate relief to get Joan and Stanley away from each other in the day, and to follow this up with respite care.

Thus the immediate practical relief offered was two days of day care at a progressive old peoples' home, where Stanley was encouraged in his piano playing to make a lively contribution. He was able to go to the same home for respite care, at first for two weeks in and six weeks at home, on a rota. Here he was able to show a different side to himself. He became less forgetful, and more business-like, helping with the washing up. This gave Joan a taste of freedom, but not yet enough. She was still feeling bad about the sherry. The respite care was increased to three weeks in and three weeks out, thus stabilising the situation. A move to a two-bedroomed flat also helped.

The social worker was gradually able to undertake counselling about the feelings of grief Joan still had on the death of her first husband whom she dearly loved, and about her guilt in not being able to cope with Stanley. She became able to share the strain with social services. The social worker was left with a feeling of uncertainty about who her client was, a kind of balancing act being required between the needs of both of the Fitches. Each person could well have been entered on the case load as a separate case, in view of the time and attention each required. Ongoing counselling offered the opportunity to explore further areas; regular reviews at the old peoples' home are part of the necessary monitoring of the situation. In this and the following story, religious belief played a significant part in what does, or does not seem possible for the client to accept. We often ignore that aspect, but as people get older many return to, or strengthen their religious views.

CASE STUDY 2.3 – FAMILY KHAN

A Punjabi family arranged to have the husband's mother brought to Britain so that he could care for her. It was not appropriate for the son to care for her but it became too much for the daughter-in-law, who was admitted to psychiatric hospital with a nervous breakdown, and the problems were referred to the local area social service office. In discussion with the son about possible services it was discovered that hospital day care could be arranged, but it would be humiliating for the family to have an ambulance call at the home. Even if a taxi service were provided to take his mother it would not help as there were no other Muslim women there and she would not get any stimulation. A Punjabi speaking volunteer was suggested to sit in, but this was not acceptable as the family did not want to commit themselves to a regular time for the volunteer to call.

Thus many cultural barriers on both sides had to be explored, between what was acceptable in a strict Muslim household, and what social services felt they could provide. In this case no service then available was suitable, and in the end sadly the family sent the elderly person back to Pakistan, to relatives there. A day centre staffed by Muslim people, including some women, might provide a solution in this case. There used to be a 'chicken and egg' situation that complicated the provision of appropriate services for ethnic minority elderly people. Without a demand for services, no services were thought to be necessary. Without the possibility of appropriate services there would be no take up or demand. Fortunately ways of breaking into this cycle have begun to be identified (Mossadeq and Froggatt, 1988).

These cases demonstrate that social care planning involves far more than slotting in occasional services piece meal, as they are available. It involves careful placing of the services to meet and match the client's family network as far as possible. The ongoing monitoring and support of services in a planned way is also required. It may seem risky to start investing so much time and effort to obtain a better quality of life for a person at the margin of coping, but once the framework of social care planning has been established other aspects of social work and health service provision can be woven in.

Summary

This chapter has tried to establish a perspective for undertaking social work practice from a social services department, in liaison with colleagues from other occupations. The necessity for under-taking a bio-psychosocial assessment, before starting to plan any social care has been explored, with the help of case examples.

The next chapter examines some of the statutory responsibilities carried by Social Services Departments in England and Wales, Scotland and Northern Ireland, and areas of particular difficulty in carrying out those responsibilities to care for vulnerable elderly people.

3

Areas of Particular Complexity

The previous chapter set out the framework for social work intervention for a social services department. This chapter outlines statutory responsibilities for vulnerable elderly people. This is followed by an exploration of certain circumstances which may present a particular set of difficulties for clients, their families and the social worker. Extra knowledge and skill may be needed. These areas are the relatively common experiences of loss and bereavement, ageing in a strange country, mental infirmity, issues around sexuality, alcoholism, and the problems presented if elder abuse is suspected.

Statutory social work

The legal framework within which services for elderly people must be provided is less extensive than that for child care. This was recognised in a survey of the legal position (Age Concern, 1986). It was hoped that more would be done by legislation to impose on local authorities a duty to consider, assess and intervene 'Where there are elderly people in need of some support or advice in order to prevent or postpone personal or social deterioration or breakdown – necessitating their removal to institutional care' (Age Concern, 1986, p. 128). Areas of particular concern were where elderly people were in danger of self neglect, abuse, or inability to manage their own affairs because of mental infirmity.

The statutory responsibilities of social service authorities for elderly people cover three main areas of provision, residential accommodation, domiciliary services and protective powers for

36

those most vulnerable. The position for England and Wales will be described first, and then the legislative provisions for Scotland and Northern Ireland.

Legislation in England and Wales

Residential accommodation   The local authority may provide residential accommodation for persons who 'by reason of age are in need of care and attention which is not otherwise available to them'. This power in the National Assistance Act (1948) Part III also allows the authority to buy in places in private and voluntary homes. The extent of provision varies between authorities (Audit Commission, 1985).

Domiciliary services   These are provided under three major pieces of legislation. The Health Services and Public Health Act (1968) Section 45 is that which empowers the local authority to carry out many of the major services for elderly people, home helps, laundry service, meals on wheels, warden services, boarding out, aids and adaptations, and advice, information and social work support. This act does not give a clear entitlement to the services; provision in any particular case depends on sufficient resources being available.

The Chronically Sick and Disabled Persons' Act (1970), offers permissive powers to assist those of any age with a disability. There is a duty to provide aids adaptations, holidays, telephones and meals within any financial constraints which the authority is under. The Disabled Persons' (Services Consultation and Representation) Act (1986), added to the powers of local authorities but has been implemented only slowly. When assessing the needs of a disabled person (including an elderly person with disabilities) who receives a substantial amount of care regularly from someone not employed by the local authority, the authority is required to: 'have regard to the ability of that person to continue to provide help on a regular basis'.

Protective powers   Where people are vulnerable because of the extent of their mental infirmities, severe physical disability, or extreme age, there are statutory responsibilities for their personal care and their financial protection. These are discussed in some detail, because the exercise of these powers involves a careful professional judgement in the interests of the client and others in the support network.

The most controversial of these responsibilities involves the compulsory removal from home of an elderly person under Section 47 of that same Act. This has to be carried out in conjunction with the Community Physician of the Health Authority. This Act allows that adults can be forcibly placed in institutional care 'to secure the necessary care and attention if they are:

1   'suffering from grave chronic disease or being aged, infirm, or physically incapacitated, are living in unsanitary conditions;
2   unable to devote to themselves and are not receiving from other persons proper care and attention.'

The two main sets of circumstances to which the Act is normally applied relate first to mental disorder and secondly to self-neglect over a long period. In the former case provisions of the 1982 Mental Health Act such as guardianship may be more appropriate. Concern arises in the second case as there may well be a conflict of interest between the rights of an elderly person to live an eccentric independent life, and the rights of family or neighbours to be protected from hazards for example of vermin or fire. Section 47 is used sparingly, perhaps only on 200 people a year (Age Concern, 1986, p. 39-49). It is used to different degrees in different authorities, which indicates that some have found a way to avoid this particular form of compulsory removal. It is opposed by the British Association of Social workers on the grounds that it is ageist and does not adequately safeguard the rights of clients (Marshall, 1988, p. 20).

An alternative power to Section 47 is offered in the Mental Health Act 1983 (S.7–10 Guardianship). Here two doctors must support the application to be made by an approved social worker or nearest relative. It is effectively a social service order as the authority becomes the Guardian and can require the person to live in a certain residential establishment, to accept treatment, occupation or training, and to receive visits from a doctor or social worker. This order lasts for six months initially, and the person can appeal to a Mental Health Tribunal.

Elderly people with mental impairment who can no longer manage their own affairs may need assistance from a social worker in protecting their finances by consultation with the Court of Protection, under the Mental Health Act 1983. It may be necessary to take out a

Power of Attorney, or an Enduring Power of Attorney (Age Concern, 1986, p. 76–86). The Court of Protection exists for people who really cannot manage their own affairs, and have some reserves of property, capital, or income to handle. There is sometimes reluctance by solicitors and relatives to use the procedure, but it can be invaluable. In 1985, 22545 people were under its protection (Age Concern, 1986, p. 76). A Receiver is usually appointed if there are assets over £5000. The Power of Attorney is given to a relative or solicitor to act as Attorney or donee, but this power ought to lapse if the donor is mentally incapacitated, and the Court of Protection should step in. Many Attorneys do continue to act for incapacitated donors. However, to remedy this widespread misuse of the Power of Attorney, in 1985 the Enduring Power of Attorney Act was passed. This was intended to help elderly people no longer fully capable, but still with sufficient understanding to create the power. Once the Attorney thinks the person is mentally incapable he/she should register the Enduring Power of Attorney with the Court of Protection.

Where relatives have an expectation of ultimate benefit from any property or capital, the situation becomes even more complex. The emotional problems associated with a possible conflict of interest may need to be recognised. The Attorney, who has the power to use resources to buy in domestic or residential care, has a considerable responsibility.

Legal provisions in Scotland

The general provisions for residential and domiciliary services are enacted in the Social Work (Scotland) Act (1968). Residential Homes provided by the regional councils are known as Part iv accommodation. The Chronically Sick and Disabled Persons' Act (1970) and the Disabled Persons' (Services Advice and Representation) Act (1986) also apply to Scotland.

There is different legislation for mentally impaired elderly people. Guardianship is provided for in the Mental Health (Scotland) Act (1984), Section 37 Guardianship. The powers for compulsory removal are given under the National Assistance Act (1948), S.47. Those with impaired powers to manage financially can give a verbal mandate to another person, or a written mandate, creating a power of attorney. This should lapse if a sufferer can no longer direct his/ her own affairs. A Curator Bonis, which occurs in Judicial Factor Acts, can be appointed under S.92–3 of the Mental Health (Scotland) Act (1984). This is a financial manager, usually a solicitor or accountant, who charges for services, and this is appropriate where there is a reasonable amount of capital. However, the curator has a duty to the estate rather than to the ward, and may save money, not spend it to benefit the ward. Nor can the curator direct where the ward should live. When ordinary people with little or no capital are incapable of handling benefits, anyone can apply to the Department of Social Security to act on his/her behalf, under the Social Security (Claims and Payments) Regulations (1987).

Thus there is an unsatisfactory division between financial protection and the personal welfare of the sufferer, in Scots law. Scottish Action on Dementia have recommended proposals similar to the Scottish system of Childrens' Hearings, for those with mental impairment, to improve the situation (Boyd, 1988).

Northern Ireland: social service provision

The framework for services in Northern Ireland arose through the integration of health and personal services in 1973, reorganising these services into four joint boards. The intention was to focus on programmes of care to meet the needs of different client groups, and to plan services jointly. These administrative arrangements broke down some of the barriers in co-ordinating services, but grassroots co-operation has not appeared to be necessarily easier than elsewhere in Great Britain. Where services have been jointly planned it is easier to maintain them. The Area boards which have set up multidisciplinary teams to consider the care of elderly people have focused on information gathering, producing policy advice on multidisciplinary problems and future needs (Birrell and Williamson, 1983).

General social welfare provisions for elderly people are enacted in the Health and Person Social Services Act 1977. This includes provision of residential accommodation, domiciliary support and the registration of homes provided for those in need. For mentally impaired elderly people the relevant legislation for Guardianship and the Court of Protection occurs in the Mental Health (Northern

Ireland) Order (1986). Protection of Property and Removal Powers are enacted in the Health and Personal Social Services (Northern Ireland) Act 1972 schedule [b]. Disabled people are provided for through the Chronically Sick and Disabled Persons' (Northern Ireland) Act (1978).

In carrying out statutory duties for elderly people in all parts of the United Kingdom a social worker must be as fully informed as possible of all relevant circumstances. A very careful assessment is needed. This must include recognition of the impact of particular events and circumstances, some of which are now described in more detail.

Loss and bereavement

Work with vulnerable elderly people frequently involves recognition of the significant losses in their lives. Referral often follows on a bereavement or a failure in health. Coping with loss and sustaining morale is not easy, requiring considerable courage.

Later old age does involve a series of losses for many people which have to be surmounted, whether it is loss of physical activity or sight, hearing, loss of house or home, or the death of those close in affection. It takes time, patience and resilience to work through losses; sometimes a further loss triggers off grief for an insufficiently mourned event. The death of a sister might involve deep grief, part of which might be for the much earlier death of a small sister. The cumulative effect of losses should be borne in mind. One of the functions of later life is dealing with and coming to terms with many earlier experiences to review life and evaluate it. Some people have an element of spirituality within the emotional aspects of life which should not be forgotten, but which is easily overlooked in a secular society. Very old people have lived most of their lives in a society where more people attended services of worship and found religious belief of value to them.

Whatever the personal beliefs of the worker, the meaning of religion to the client should be noted, and efforts made to facilitate whatever religious expression is helpful. We may realise that a Muslim needs a place to roll out his prayer mat five times a day. We need to see the comfort a confused old person derives from holding a prayer book or rosary. Religious beliefs help some people to make ultimate sense of loss and death.

Thus understanding the social world of vulnerable elderly people involves exploring the meaning of death in a personal way. Death sets a frame around life, gives it a context, adding a sharpness and purpose to each stage. To contemplate death may be scary, but for those with a strong religious faith it can be almost exciting. The fear of protracted, wearisome and painful dying can be stronger. Approaching death should be viewed in it own personal cultural and religious perspective for the person concerned. A helpful discussion of ways to care for dying people of different faiths has been compiled (Neuberger, 1987).

Grieving for a person is hard physical work, following a fairly regular set of stages (Parkes, 1986). The phase of shock and somatic distress is normally followed by a restless searching, mixed with anger and irritability towards the deceased, and any one else who might be blamed for the present distress. This stage involves ambivalence, love and anger competing for priority. There is an urge to recapture the missing person in some way by hanging on to memories, and treasures. In normal grief, within about six months, but this may take considerably longer, the claims of friends and family still left should reassert themselves, and more normal social relationships be re-established. Relatives need help with grieving, for past relationships in the family can easily become crystalised at death. Acute grief at the death of one parent may inhibit a family for caring for the surviving spouse. An extreme example of this occurred when a hospital social worker was asked to see a family who refused to allow a newly bereaved husband to leave hospital to attend his wife's funeral, as they felt angrily that he had contributed to her unexpected death with his demands. The social worker tried to mediate without success in the available time.

Elders from minority groups may experience particular dimensions of loss which will be further explored in the following section.

Becoming old in a strange country

Within the multiracial society of the United Kingdom an increasing proportion of people will become old from among ethnic minority groups. From the year 2000 onwards it is estimated there will be 104000 from the Indian subcontinent (South Asia), 100000 Caribbean, 125000 from the Far East (Chinese) (Norman, 1985).

In addition there are smaller groups of minority elders, some of whom came as refugees from East Europe, Kenya or Vietnam. Cypriot and Irish elders came for employment in earlier years and have stayed (ibid.). Is it possible to begin to understand the difficulties minority elders face, those of ordinary ageing compounded by extra factors? First, poverty and inner city deprivation is a most important aspect. Some who came in as dependents are not eligible for income support. It has been shown that 10 per cent of the 400 people interviewed in Birmingham had given a lower age to gain admission to Britain, and now cannot gain a pension at the proper time (Bhalla and Blakemore, 1981).

Secondly, the difficulties of elderly people from different backgrounds are exacerbated by the incipient and institutional racism and abuse in our society, a degree of hostility which had not been expected. Institutionalised racism manifests itself in insensitive service provision in health and social services, with barriers around language, the pattern of family names and vocabulary.

Thirdly, the myth that ethnic minority elders inevitably prefer to be and always are looked after by their own is being exposed (Grant, 1988). The reality is that people of all groups face similar economic pressures to work and obtain adequate housing. The pressures of intergenerational living are compounded by climatic differences. For example both domestic overcrowding and cultural expectations encourage elderly Asian men to leave the house during the day (Bhalla and Blakemore, 1981). As public shopping arcades lend themselves to situations of abuse it is important that they have somewhere warm to go; one example of a voluntary initiative is that Bradford Council of Mosques has set up a day centre for retired older men. However voluntary groups lack the funds to do as much as they would like in providing comfortable well staffed centres.

If services are to be provided by indigenous voluntary bodies or statutory agencies, there needs to be an acceptance of different cultural and religious traditions involving diet, food preparation and meals, toilet and ablution provisions, and privacy for regular prayer times. Then ethnic minority elders might feel comfortable in accepting help from outside the family and community. There is a further distinction to be made between what is socially admissable and what is acceptable (see case study 2.3).

The self perceptions of people growing old in a different country are somewhat neglected in research. It is surely self-evident that whatever role they might have expected to perform in the family is likely to be changed, by being alienated from their roots. Isolation, rejection, dishonour and disrespect might be expected at different times. However much the family cling to their culture and security, the younger generation at work and school are grappling with a different set of realities; the wisdom of the older family member may be less acceptable. Instead of dispensing advice and controlling the purse strings, elders may find themselves servicing the young family by doing shopping and escorting the children to school.

Fifthly, the disappointment at not returning home becomes another loss. Language differences may increase with extreme age as the second language is forgotten (Rack, 1982). A reaction to these difficulties may be withdrawal, apathy, or acting out behaviour.

This may seem a very gloomy picture, and it is perhaps exaggerated, but leaders of minority groups are encouraging social workers at all levels to make adequate and appropriate provision. The need is now well established (Mossadeq and Froggatt, 1988). Cultural and religious differences are likely to remain for they are about identity and belief, rather than habit. Satisfaction for elderly people comes from being part of a cohesive group who know the rules, the politics and the history. A family systems approach to work with minority groups must take account of all these factors.

Sexuality and sexual problems

Social workers are sometimes asked to assist families where there are difficulties around the expression of sexuality in an older family member. Difficulties arise for the individual and those around him/her. Society is ambivalent about recognising that elderly people have a legitimate wish to continue to express their sexuality in physical ways. It is an aspect of ageism that old age is seen as asexual.

This ties in with a generally romantic view of sexual expression denying this to anyone with any degree of physical or mental impairment (Strean, 1983). Sexuality involves much more than sexual intercourse. Vitality and creativity flow from this source, as does the need for close body warmth, touching, and physical contact with another human being.

While recognising that successful sexual relations in later life depended to some extent on earlier satisfactory sexual expression the study known as the Starr–Weiner Report (Starr and Bakur-Weiner, 1982) confirmed that 'Older adults are interested in sex, think about it, desire it, engage in it with the same frequency that Kinsey reported for forty year-olds.'

This study was based on an open-ended questionnaire completed by 800 older adults aged 60–91. 35 per cent were males, 65 per cent were females; 48 per cent married, 37 per cent widowed, 11 per cent divorced. It is clear from this survey that elderly people continue to need the affirmation of self which sexual expression can bring. As respondents said: 'Being loved, touched and wanted fills a need.' 'It makes me feel more certain of myself.' Seventy-five per cent of respondents said that sex was the same or better now than when younger.

Thus our societal reluctance to acknowledge the sexual needs of older people can create difficulties. In residential homes a couple who want to live together and express themselves sexually have in the past received ridicule if not hostility, instead of facilitated support.

Other sexual behaviour can occasionally present problems as described by a psychologist.

> There are the more frankly pathological behaviours – the effect of organic deterioration in the brain which sometimes results in sexual disinhibition. In both sexes compulsive public masturbation is one of the commonest examples referred for treatment (Skinner, 1988).

Coping with these problems is not easy.

> Balancing the rights and therapeutic needs of the elderly to sexual expression with the requirement to protect other residents from unwelcome and possibly exploitive situations, produces management problems which defy simple prescriptive solutions (ibid.).

Social workers together with formal and informal carers and family need to be able to discuss the sexual needs of elderly people, particularly where behaviour presents problems. This discussion should include other professionals in the multidisciplinary team and may need to start with a recognition of their own feelings, before meeting with the old person concerned. Then one might recognise the legitimacy of sexual expression and try to find more socially acceptable ways to release that energy.

Mental impairment

The lives of vulnerable elderly people are made more complex when there is mental impairment, as there is a general anxiety about their capacity to cope with themselves or the environment. The term 'confusion' is easily used about an elderly person who seems to be 'losing his grip'. This term covers a number of causes, ranging from acute infectious illness, mental illness, organic brain failure, or a combination of these (Marshall, 1988; Gearing *et al.*, 1988). In discussing the interactions of mental illnesses and brain failure Gray and Isaacs (1979) showed that illnesses such as depression, psychosis and neurosis do continue to occur in old age but are more likely to recur than appear for the first time. A strong reactive element has been identified in later life depression (Murphy, 1983).

Most old people retain their intellectual capacity except for minor short-term memory lapses for which protective strategies are often developed – making lists, sticking to routine. However a sizeable proportion of the very elderly population, perhaps as much as 20 per cent of people over 80 (Norman, 1987a), do experience mental impairment of increasing severity, affecting memory, reason, self-awareness, and behaviour. One form of static impairment has been identified as Alzheimer's Disease, based on organic changes in the cells in the brain. A similar effect is experienced by those who have fluctuating or arteriosclerotic dementia, resulting from very small clots in the blood supply to the brain. Whatever the cause the effect of the dementing type of brain failure is devastating at times for both the sufferer and the carer. The loss of personality along with the total loss of short-term memory is very exhausting to live with. Close consultation with the general practitioner, or psychogeriatrician is advisable to assist in assessment and treatment.

For social workers the priorities in working with sufferers are:

1   Respecting their rights and responsibilities as full members of society, applying principles of self-determination for as long as possible (Marshall, 1988, pp. 9, 12–14).
2   Where it is clear a person has some deficits in functioning then an advocate should be appointed, a relative, friend, solicitor, or occasionally the social worker. Services from social workers should in some cases have an element of protection.
3   Ensuring a stimulating caring environment where basic needs

for warmth and cleanliness are matched by affection and concern (see Chapter 6 for working in a residential setting).
4 Supporting the family and carers who may not be able to go on
giving the very demanding twenty-four hour care needed in the
later stages of the illness.

This kind of work can be achieved with someone who is mentally
impaired by using skills that build trust, and trying to understand
the meaning of the experience in the light of the person's past
history. Someone with early stages of brain failure can be very
aware of it, and anxious about what is happening to him/her. This
may mean becoming even more rigid and defensive about receiving
help. Wasser (1966) detailed the approach needed, to move in
slowly admitting that we all have times of independence, and times
of feeling helpless. It takes strength of character to admit one needs
help. She explored protective services for elderly people, advocating
a proactive stance, taking the initiative to give the client a taste of a
service, on the assumption that saying 'no' will be the automatic
response to something threatening (Wasser, 1971). The emotional
feelings of people with advanced brain failure may be intact, but
somewhat free floating as people and objects become no longer
recognisable.

There are two sorts of risk to take into account in planning care
with a client and family where there is mental impairment (Davies
and Challis, 1986, p. 327). These are, first, the *process risk* by which
a person with brain failure is likely to become increasingly self-
neglectful and disordered in time with reduced skills to cope.
Secondly, the *event risk* is the likelihood of such a person forgetting
to light the gas, switch off the electric cooker, lock the doors, or turn
off the bath tap. Carrying through a sequence of actions becomes
increasingly hard. They also identify the concept of patterning care
to take advantage of a person's routine to send in a helper 'when it
get's dark' to prepare a light meal before bed. This time would vary
with the season, thus using imagination and flexibility to help such a
client retain some autonomy.

These notes about social work practice where there is mental
impairment cannot begin to be comprehensive; skills in this area are
developing fast. Marshall (1988, p. 31) identifies a number of skills
emphasising assessment and interagency work, as we have already
done. With dementia sufferers it is crucially important to work

closely with the family network, all the formal and informal carers and family, whether in the community, or following admission to a residential home. The highest professional standards are needed to cope with the complexity of issues.

The immediate family and carers go through a chronic grief process alongside the need to go on caring for and sustaining a person who is slipping away, cognitively, behaviourally and emotionally. Affection and dread are mixed in ambivalence, grief becomes guilt, and often a disgust factor at the kind of tasks to be undertaken compounds the pain (Ungerson, 1987). Thus a counselling role for supporters, offering a safe space to acknowledge these feelings is an essential part of social work practice in this kind of circumstance.

Alcohol related problems

There is some evidence that alcoholism in old age is more common than generally realised (Butler and Lewis, 1982, p. 106). Alcohol depresses the nervous system, and taken in excess impairs intellectual functioning. Alcohol abuse can present as mental infirmity, with times of poor memory, incontinence, depression and shakiness, so it is particularly important to distinguish between these two conditions if possible (Goodman and Ward, 1988).

Consumption by elderly people seems to be of three sorts:

1   a regular glass of beer or sherry to give a high spot to the day as a morale booster, and following a long held habit (Roberts, 1988);
2   problem drinkers who live on to old age, perhaps having started in midlife;
3   some people turn to excessive alcohol in later life in reaction to depression, grief, loneliness, boredom or pain. Elderly widowers have the highest rate of alcoholism of all groups (Butler and Lewis, 1982).

Identifying alcohol related problems may not be easy. Complaints of insomnia, impotence, or gout, or the sudden onset of a confusional state could be indicators. More obvious signs might be a large pile of empty bottles, the smell of drink, or unwashed glasses. One study exploring alcohol and drug abuse among elderly people, found there was evidence this could be a major problem. The presence of a principal supporter was invaluable to help keep someone off abuse and receiving treatment (Bradford Brown and Chiang, 1983–4). Depression and a diminution in self care were noted in the few cases identified in the Kent Community Care project (Davies and Challis, 1986).

Here again the support network is crucial in trying to help someone with alcohol related problems, as one needs to reconnect the person to a social network which offers interest and stimulation in lieu of alcohol. This is where family work could be useful helping the whole family to understand the part alcohol has come to play in the life of the vulnerable elderly person, the pattern of abuse, the defensiveness about it, and the likely outcome.

Elder abuse

This has been defined as 'systematic and continuous abuse of an elderly person by the carer, often though not always a relative on whom the elderly person is *dependent* for care' (Cloke, 1983, p. 2). The incidence of elder abuse is hard to quantify. This term is preferred as it signifies ill-treatment of a person. It is difficult to research as it is behaviour which takes place in a domestic setting involving powerless people. It is a symptom of ageism reflecting the low status of dependent elderly people including those in residential homes. It reflects the inviolability of family life that in our society helps to mask the darker side of caring and dependency. Many social workers have known instances of actual or threatened harm to or from elderly people and their carers. Most research does involve consulting professionals (Cloke, 1983; Eastman, 1984) as it is difficult to identify abusers or victims. The definition of elder abuse has been drawn widely by Eastman (1984) to include physical abuse, threatening behaviour, neglect and abandonment, and sexual assault. Financial abuse is the exploitation of the elderly person's assets. The predisposing factors identified (Eastman, 1984, Hickey, 1981) include severe physical and mental infirmity which wears down the carer, poor communication, lack of respite care, lack of praise from the dependent person. In families where there is a predisposition to violence, especially where an adult was abused as a child by the parent, the concept of elder abuse offers a further example of the violence extended in that family towards the least powerful members.

Middle-aged adults, especially women are sometimes asked to care for parents who have been violent or sexually abusive towards them in the past. Those exploring a persons's reluctance to care should be sensitive to this possibility; present relationships are coloured by memories of what has gone before.

Old age abuse is a term that can be used more properly to refer to situations where it happens that the elderly person is abusing the carer (Case Study 4.2). This can be caused by a number of factors usually relating to the previous relationships and patterns of communication within the family. A dominant parent may entrap a more passive son and daughter into an intolerable situation, where the parent's behaviour can be physically abusive, emotionally demanding, and/or extremely manipulative.

There seems a reluctance by agencies to act in cases of physical or emotional elder abuse; it is possible that to introduce complex procedures will merely increase anxieties and exacerbate problems. Many circumstances are made intolerable as it is for lack of sufficient respite services. Many victims do not wish to complain out of loyalty or fear. A more sensitive way of handling elder abuse, including counselling and the rapid introduction of relief services could show that this phenomenon is a recognised concomitant of the excessive strains of caring, especially for mentally impaired elderly people (Traynor and Hasnip, 1984). The extension of family work to situations of elder abuse has been found helpful (Kinney *et al.*, 1988).

Abuse in residential homes can occur in both local authority and private homes. The delay in implementing an inquiry into Nye Bevan Lodge in Southwark from 1985–7 demonstrated the institutional resistance to recognising that standards of care could degenerate where physical and mental infirmity were accompanied by social powerlessness, whether as resident, or low paid care assistant.

In a review of the legal framework for intervention in elder abuse (Age Concern, 1986, pp. 32–7) it was made explicit that: 'Social service departments have very few statutory responsibilities towards elderly people, very few powers to protect, none to represent and limited resources to help' (Age Concern, 1986, p. 34).

It was proposed that the following points should be borne in mind when considering any procedures to help in cases of abuse.

1 People should be made aware of both actual and potential old age abuse, its causes and ways of preventing it.
2 More systems of help advice and support for elderly victims and their carers need to be provided.
3 Better ways of representing old people at risk of abuse should be sought and developed.
4 Better procedures for reporting cases of abuse or suspected abuse of old people need to be developed (Age Concern, 1986, p. 37)

Summary

This chapter has acknowledged that social workers have limited but significant statutory responsibilities for elderly people which have been outlined. The circumstances in which social workers are asked to intervene are likely to be complex, as many of the case studies elsewhere in the book show. There are areas of particular importance which require extra knowledge and understanding from the start. These have been explored in more depth, namely loss and bereavement, elders from ethnic minority groups, ageing in a strange country, issues around sexuality, mental infirmity, alcoholism and elder abuse.

4

Direct Social Work with Individuals

In this chapter the focus is on developing communication skills, in order to undertake face-to-face social work with clients and members of their family network, either as individuals or with two or three people together. The emphasis here is first on developing a relationship, and then on using other core skills to implement a social care plan. This involves planning the intervention and evaluating the outcome. Alternative types of direct social work are examined in which a framework is offered for the worker to plan the interaction. These are task centred work and crisis intervention. The chapter concludes with some examples of how insights gained from psychotherapy can be useful in social work practice.

The aspects of direct social work which reflect the organisational framework have been examined, case management in Chapter 2 and statutory social work in Chapter 3. A social worker may need to be aware of those aspects, and of the need to assess the client before forming a social care plan. This may include some purposeful interviews along the lines of one of the approaches to be suggested in this chapter.

Building a relationship

In social work practice the term 'relationship' is used to describe the context of the general helping activities undertaken by a social worker in interaction with a particular client. Usually the contact is for a specific purpose, and for a recognised period of time. It is built around the respect, empathy and warmth expressed by the social worker for the client. It is not necessary to like a client personally to build up a constructive relationship, but obviously it helps. The purpose of the relationship is to work together on matters of importance to the client. A social worker may have a statutory responsibility to engage the client in making a working agreement where the client is reluctant to do so. This might occur for example where an elderly person seems to those around to be failing to cope in daily life, and the situation has to be explored.

The capacity to build a relationship contains the essence of any social work interaction. In an interview the social worker needs to be able to start a conversation with someone in difficulty, who has a problem or need, and explore the matter in such a way that it seems the worker has the feel of the situation, and a grasp of the main facts. Thus empathy is the keynote. This characteristic is different from sympathy which might be described as a warm rosy glow of a feeling of identification, that lends itself to being paralysed by sorrow, overwhelmed with shared worry, and joyful too. Empathy is a more robust feeling and response. In being empathetic one is recognising the other person's feelings, and one's own answering response, but not being swamped by either. Symbolically the worker has one foot on the edge of the bog, reaching out to hold the hand of the person trampling in it, but the second foot of the worker is on firm land, to help pull the person out.

Relationships need more than empathy. They also need warmth and genuine regard (Rogers, 1967). The genuine regard or respect is demonstrated in building trust, being reliable, and taking the other person's point of view seriously, whatever one's personal opinion. Warmth should be expressed verbally, and occasionally with elderly people physical demonstrations of affection and concern are appropriate. Good communication is vital, and this will be considered further.

Communication

Communication is a two-way process. A message must be given and received. Particular skills may be needed with elderly people if there are communication difficulties. Before starting a serious conversation it is advisable to spend some time at the beginning checking ways of communication, and to establish if there is any indication of deafness, blindness, or speech difficulties. A trial run approach has been suggested particularly where it is suspected the person is hard of hearing (Deeping, 1979).

People with hearing difficulties

Start the conversation in a normal voice, and watch carefully to see how the answer matches the question. If there is an incongruous response sit in the light to assist lip reading, and repeat the question more slowly and loudly, facing the client, but without shouting or exaggeration. Sometimes gestures help. If the person is deaf, find out if there is a hearing aid, if it is being worn, is switched on, and has a good battery in it. These matters should be sorted out before assuming that the conversation is impossible, and starting to write down the information one wants to communicate. With a stranger it is not easy to explore all these aspects before starting a conversation. In severe deafness so much effort goes into making sense of what is only heard imperfectly that there is more difficulty in remembering facts, so if in any doubt it is helpful to write a note of key points, one's name, agency, and when a return visit will be paid.

Speech problems

These present a different kind of expressive difficulty, which may leave the worker feeling even more helpless. These difficulties often occur following a stroke, leaving the capacity to understand less damaged, but speaking and sometimes reading impaired. If there is a speech therapist treating the client with whom one can discuss the problem, that can be very helpful. Imaginative means of communication may need to be used. Where speech is difficult a system of hand squeezes can be used.

Drawing can also be a way to communicate. I worked with a man whose severe stroke left him only able to say 'Yes, yes, yes'. After consultation with the ward staff of the hospital where he was, and with the speech therapist, I drew a small house, his, and a large building, an old peoples' home, and asked him to point to where he wanted to go. It is important to try all possible ways to find out peoples' views on their future care, and to respect that in taking decisions.

Deaf and blind

With old people who are both deaf and blind, communication may have to be by spelling out key words on the palm of the hand, or writing letters on the forehead. Those nearest to such a person will have established some way of communicating directly. Here again effort is put into respecting the autonomy of the person who may be mentally alert, by offering choice as far as possible.

In every situation the possibility of resistance should not be overlooked. The client may not hear what is being said because it is something hard to accept. Resistance to uncomfortable news, for example a recommendation to give up one's own home, is as strongly present as in earlier life.

Core skills

Once having established some means of communication, the basic skills of negotiation, bargaining, advocacy and counselling form the stuff of every social work interaction, of however short a duration. Jordan (1987) defined a continuum of skills with negotiation as the central skill. Counselling in situations of emotional importance was at one end, and bargaining and advocacy over scarce resources was at the other. Ford (1988) by contrast believes that the insights of counselling are needed all along the way. One needs to be sensitive to the pressures on those with whom one is negotiating. Most people respond better to a positive co-operative position than to a confrontational stance.

Negotiation, bargaining and advocacy

These are valuable skills which social workers use on behalf of clients and their families and sometimes on their own behalf. Negotiation is used in situations where there is some room for manoeuvre. One cannot negotiate where an agency has clear rules, for example about the necessity for undertaking a financial assessment for an old person being admitted to local authority residential care. The assessment has to be done. Negotiation might take place about the kind of assets to be taken into account in making the assessment. Similarly it is not possible to negotiate if a client has clear rights in a situation.

In starting a negotiation it is suggested that one has a clear plan from the start identifying:

1   what is needed;
2   what resources are needed;
3   who are or might be parties to the negotiation;
4   the desired aim and the minimum aim;
5   which agencies are or might be involved;
6   what time scale is needed (Payne, 1986, pp. 49–70).

It may be necessary to negotiate with several different agencies, to put together a combination of services to sustain an elderly person at home for a particular period of time. Here one may be using negotiating skills within a relationship, with a home help organiser for example, and using counselling skill in deciding how far to push the claims of one particular client.

Bargaining can be a business-like event, exploring the ground each party wants to cover on every point at issue. The phases identified are bidding, bargaining, settling and ratifying the decision made (Payne, 1986, pp. 59–65). Social workers may be involved in bargaining with carers over how much assistance can be given to an elderly person, and how much support from services may be required to make the situation manageable for them all.

Advocacy can be a specialist activity involving either case advocacy or cause advocacy to try to reform a system (Payne, 1986). For social workers advocacy is a skill used to support a client appealing against a decision within the welfare system. It is undertaken to help balance the power between the client and the agency whom it is hoped to influence for change. Here it is important with all clients including elderly people to involve them as far as possible in the advocacy process, otherwise the client may end up feeling even more powerless, while some determined advocacy is undertaken on his/her behalf. In using these skills general planning and efficiency enhance the often finicky detailed work required with elderly clients and their relatives. The effectiveness of the arrangements made can affect the trust in the social worker, and the likelihood of services being acceptable and useful.

Counselling

Counselling involves active listening. One needs to listen carefully to any client, but older people may be more reticent about disclosure to a stranger. The spoken and unspoken words, sighs, silences and non-verbal communication must be noted. So often a person's hands, twisting a tissue, smoothing a garment, will say more about inner tension than any words.

Listening actively is demonstrated by concentration, affirming what is being said with nods, facial expressions, and short supportive or clarifying remarks to show the listener is responding. The technique of reflecting back helps the interaction: 'Let me see: have I understood you right, that your son left home before his marriage?' 'Do you find it really hard to get on with her then?' These kind of questions give the client the chance to set the worker's view straight. It also emphasises that the worker wants to get it clear. If you listen carefully, over two or three interviews you may build up an understanding of the themes and patterns of what the person is trying to say, through watching out for repetition. The events or worries that are repeated show areas that need more exploration and further discussion. In work with relatives too these techniques are useful. These core skills can be used in the ordinary kind of helping which constitutes much of the work that social workers do with clients and their families. One needs to focus on what one is trying to achieve even in brief interactions for all social work is the better for being planned and evaluated. An example of a social work interaction with an elderly client is given in the following case example of Mr Foskett. This shows the involvement of, and pressure from, concerned neighbours who are part of the family network and social support system. This concern is so often a feature of social service intervention (O'Hagan, 1986).

Case examples

CASE STUDY 4.1 – HARRY FOSKETT

A social worker was asked to visit Harry Foskett and his wife. Neighbours were concerned because a daughter with a psychiatric history, marital difficulties and debts, had moved in with the old couple. Three months later she was still there, sleeping on the sofa, and hitting the old man with his own walking stick. First the social worker went in at the old man's request, and tried to persuade the daughter and son-in-law to leave. She was a strong-willed woman, diagnosed as schizophrenic, with a quieter more passive husband. As this did not work the social worker accompanied the old man to the solicitor for a letter to evict the daughter.

About this time Mrs Foskett slipped on the floor and broke her hip, dying shortly afterwards. Having supported the old man in getting his daughter successfully evicted, the social worker embarked on weekly counselling sessions with two aims:

1 Counselling about his grief and his wife's death, in a low key way until he could talk about how he felt over her death. This shared grieving culminated in a visit they paid together nine months later to the crematorium where she was buried.
2 The maintenance of his spirit and motivation. His mobility was poor because of arthritis, but his neighbours shopped, and he cleaned and cooked. He managed with twice weekly meals on wheels, and social work support. At that stage he felt alive and in control. If a home help had been put in he would probably have gone down hill very fast.

The social worker identified the objectives for counselling, and the clarity of the plan helped to make the sessions an acceptable service to the client. This is an example of using social work time as a resource rather than day care or a home help. Counselling in this case helped a client to retain his sense of identity and purpose. By contrast an example of how counselling can be interwoven with social care planning is demonstrated in further discussion of Joan Fitch, whose problems have already been referred to in case study 2.2.

CASE STUDY 4.2 – JOAN FITCH

While Stanley's needs were met and Joan was offered some relief in respite care, it was not enough. She was still seeking some further ease of tension in drinking sherry to an extent that worried her. Regular counselling sessions were offered by the social worker and accepted. It was agreed to explore several issues. These were the feelings of loss at the death of her first husband, which she had not yet worked through, her sense of guilt at letting social services help out, and her feeling of remorse at the kind of marriage she could offer Stanley. She adopted a nurse role rather than a wife. She refused to let him touch her sexually, but she cared for his appearance, kept him active and stimulated, managed his beer consumption and dealt with all money matters.

There was some role dissonance in the expectations of each side in this marriage, which made it likely that some kind of counselling help would be required at intervals. The six-monthly reviews of respite care at the residential home provided a focus for monitoring the level and type of support needed at any stage. In evaluating this case the social worker thought that it was possible to negotiate the appropriate amount of respite care in good time, because social work involvement had included counselling and the situation had been thoroughly explored. By contrast much social work intervention occurs as a result of what appears to be an emergency. The difficulty of working in an atmosphere of crisis will be explored next.

Crisis intervention

The theory underpinning crisis intervention is of particular relevance to social work practice with old people and their families. Frequently a crisis is precipitated by some sudden change in health or behaviour, of the elderly person or a carer. In a thoughtful exploration of the relevance of Caplan's crisis theory (1961) for social work practice, O'Hagan proposed that the chaotic situations which frequently present themselves in a social service department require a different understanding of the nature of a crisis and the part played by a social worker in resolving it.

A crisis may be caused by an actual or threatened loss or hazardous event, which challenges and outstrips the actual coping capacity of the client and/or the family (Caplan, 1961). Usually after a period of considerable discomfort and attempted solutions some apparent answer is found which may be successful or unsuccessful in meeting the long-term interests of the client. In the intervening period, the four to six weeks during which the search for a solution takes place, the client and family may well be ready to explore the situation fully, facing the impact of earlier successful or unsuccessfully re-solved crises as part of the existing crisis.

O'Hagan (1986) considers that this leisurely view of a social worker having four to six weeks to explore a crisis with a client does not match up to the experience in social service departments. This is particularly so in the 'plea for removal' type of crisis, when friends and neighbours get together to insist that a person is a danger to him/herself, or the community. He has clarified this way of working very helpfully (ibid.).

He suggests that the social worker has to enter into those situations of panic, chaos and trauma, and somehow offer hope. As described more fully in Chapter 6, the social worker has somehow to avoid becoming part of the problem, by being identified in the client's eyes as ganging up with neighbours and family.

Sometimes vulnerable old people are caught up in a more general crisis such as a major road or rail accident, or other disaster. Here the response of the social worker must be to use appropriate communication skills, coupled with a broader understanding of the impact of a disaster on all involved. This includes allowing plenty of time to talk through the impact of events.

Task-centred work

There is increasing evidence that one particular form of direct social work, task-centred work, is particularly useful in working with elderly clients and their families (Goldberg and Connelly, 1982, p. 88; Coulshed, 1988). This type of work, developed by Reid and Epstein (1977), showed that even with relationship problems, short-term focused work produced much better results than long-term open-ended work. Since that study, increasing use has been made of the task-centred approach, which targets seven problem areas in which change is possible:

interpersonal conflict;
dissatisfaction with social relations;
role performance;
problems in social transition;
reactive emotional distress;
problems with formal organisations;
inadequate resources.

The particular value of task-centred work is that it is based on an intention to form an agreement or contract between the client and the worker, thus freeing the client from the burden of always being a grateful recipient. This particularly assists those elderly clients who may be resentful at times that they appear to need help.

Secondly, the client and worker identify the main problem together, or put the problems in priority order, deciding together where to start. It does help if the first task is achievable, for example to telephone the Housing Department, rather than to get rehoused.

Thirdly, a time limit is set, usually three months, within which it is hoped to achieve the goals. Fourthly, in setting out the contract which may be oral or written, the activities to be undertaken are sorted out into individual tasks, and allocated between the worker and the client. It is important that the client's first task is one in which success is highly probable, as nothing succeeds like success in this way of working.

Fifthly, the process of reviewing progress and reestablishing the next round of tasks allows any achievement to be reinforced. This is a good way to evaluate the effectiveness of social work intervention, a significant aspect, as efficiency becomes increasingly important within a social service department.

There are some ways in which this approach should be adapted for elderly clients (Fortune and Rathbone McCuan, 1981). It is suggested that it is helpful not to emphasise the problem or disability, as some old people are reluctant to face their inability to continue to cope independently. The social worker should undertake some of the tasks so that progress is made. Notes or memory aides could be made of tasks to be done, or tasks accomplished, and copies left with the client as a reminder. It helps to emphasise the elderly person's past strengths and coping abilities. Lastly, where there is a reluctance on the part of the client to involve relatives, whether siblings or adult children, it might be appropriate for the social worker to become more directive, and take the initiative in this negotiation.

The task-centred approach is not seen as being particularly useful in areas where there is a mental health problem, or severe mental impairment, where long-term dependency is envisaged, or where the client is unable to accept that there is a problem to be dealt with and worked on. Goldberg and Connelly (1982, p. 88) suggest the wide variety of situations where this way of working can be helpful, ranging from short-term grief work, to a change of residence, or the too close involvement of caring relatives who might need additional support.

These examples are in addition to tasks such as mobilising and creating resources to meet specific needs. The fact that monitoring and evaluation are built into this way of working adds to the efficient use of resources, particularly by breaking up activities and the focus of work in a long-term situation.

CASE STUDY 4.3 – MR JIM MUNRO

This case demonstrates the kind of situation where this type of work is helpful. A request came to a social service department to assist Jim Munro, who was to be rehoused in a council flat. He was a man of 73, old for his years, who had been neglecting himself in his very bare rented flat. The social worker who took on the referral found him somewhat embarrassed by his present circumstances, and the degree to which he had let himself go. She recognised this and took care to build up his self-confidence by involving him at every stage of the planning for the move. First they had to prepare a claim for payment for furniture, bedding and carpets from the Department of Health and Social Security. She arranged with the friend beside whom he was being rehoused to do his shopping on a regular basis. The day before the move Mr Munro was outfaced by the prospect of it, and needed to spend time talking through his feelings at leaving the old flat. And then arrangements had to be made to transport his cats as well as himself to the new flat.

By discussion, planning and reviewing the achievements together, the worker was able to ensure that Mr Munro kept some hold on the situation, even though she acted as his agent to a large extent in undertaking most of the tasks. She was able to help him share his anxiety about the risk of moving, and this made it more manageable. So often people become almost paralysed by the apparent enormity of the tasks to be undertaken, that the only way to give the necessary support is to help them to partialise the tasks.

An interesting example of task-centred work in an old people's home showed ways which could be helpful to residential workers, or health care teams in hospital, to work on adjustment to residential life, or the hospital care the client might experience (Dierking *et al.*, 1980). Behavioural elements can be worked into a task-centred programme, teaching someone who has lived a rather isolated life how to begin to make conversation again.

Social workers who find practice with old people somewhat daunting, as discussed earlier may find this way of working is helpful. It gives a sharper focus to an interview, helping the worker cope with the flood of reminiscence which a lonely old person may release. Working with carers and helpers can be done in a task-centred way, helping to partialise the difficulties and problems they may be facing, to find a solution bit by bit.

Brief counselling in loss and death

As people become older, the experience of the death of close relatives and friends occurs more frequently; multiple losses of different sorts, with accompanying periods of bereavement can also cause considerable sadness and sometimes depression. It is helpful to encourage clients and relatives to talk of these feelings. In doing so they will not only be dealing with grief and loss, but also rethinking their own daily living arrangements. Sometimes we can focus too much on practical arrangements, and think of grief as a normal concomitant of old age. This is to undervalue the grief work, which could be assisted by listening to the stories of the person, the events of the death, and the pain of the loss being experienced.

However as the following case shows, not every one needs to share mourning.

CASE STUDY 3.4 – MR HAMISH

A social worker was called to see an old man in his seventies who had been taken to the police station for shoplifting a tin of corned beef. He was very worried, afraid of the shame if his daughter got to know. The worker saw him twice, offering a counselling service. He was an incredibly fit old man, whose wife had died a year ago. He tramped the moors every day. He did not want any services and did not see counselling help as a service a social worker might offer, nor did he want to share any grieving for his wife. The worker accepted that at that point he did not require any more help, and terminated the contract, leaving her address. Here she was recognising the client's right to choose what help was acceptable, and she had also made a careful assessment of the situation at that time.

CASE STUDY 3.5 – WORKING WITH A DYING PERSON

By contrast a vivid example of brief counselling with a dying old man was given by Hunter (1983). An old man in hospital used her visits to work out his own sense of timing. He missed death in the trenches in the First World War, had a daughter who died young, and he was now in hospital separated from his wife. He worked out when he was born, wanted to know the time of day, when the worker would return and when he would see his wife again. All this focus on time gave him a sense of peace, and he died an hour after the worker had left him. 'His impressive use of time culminated in finality' (ibid.).

It is not often that social workers are given the opportunity to work closely with people at the end of their lives. In order to accept and welcome those chances it helps to have worked out in thinking and preparatory supervision one's own feelings about dying. In these examples we see death and bereavement, together with other losses as an important aspect of work in counselling elderly people.

Psychotherapy

Those who are practising psychotherapy with older people have valuable experience which social workers can adapt for use in working with elderly clients. There are several approaches which are helpful, given that, as described already, elderly people's hearing, eyesight, and memory may be less active than previously and their responses may be marginally slower.

Goodstein (1982) identified a number of points worth remembering in this context. First, anticipate the losses old people are likely to have experienced and ask about them directly. These are part of the agenda for any discussion and the old person needs reassurance that such experience is recognised as important.

Secondly, there is 'a need to be more giving' of oneself than normally in a psychotherapeutic or counselling relationship. The older person may be looking to the therapist or social worker to replace some earlier loss, such as a daughter, son, sibling or spouse, and will appreciate a sharing of feeling or experience much more. The time spent together might be given over to sharing a game of dominoes, or cards, knitting, or having a quick drink, if the circumstances were right. This suggestion is not dissimilar to the recommended way of getting closer to children by working together over a third object, such as a drawing, or a jigsaw puzzle.

Thirdly it helps to be specific about the tasks to be undertaken and the time to be allocated to them. This means that suggestions about sharing activities as outlined above do not lead to unrealistic expectations, and that the advantages of doing task-centred work can be mobilised.

The social worker or counsellor should be prepared to include the role of health co-ordinator, holding the threads of the various aspects of health care which can get confusing and complex. Here in Britain we see a major role as key worker, or care manager, co-ordinating welfare services as well as health care.

Goodstein (1982) emphasised that it was essential to be scrupulously honest, along with this listening patiently and respectfully. Contact and rapport could be established and maintained by a more open sharing of feelings, whether laughter or tears, than one might usually expect. There was a need to reach out and put a hand on a person's shoulder, take her/his arm, hold a hand, thus increasing the repertoire of non-verbal communication with older people.

There is a need to go on being touched, to receive affection and recognition in this way all through life.

A further area of insight suggested (ibid.) is to recognise and respect the ideal or inner age of the person; how old does he/she feel inside today? Is it always the same? Which age was the most important? This may conflict with the chronological age, and the person may switch backwards and forwards from one age to another, so it requires alertness to work out what the person is feeling. One should also try to foster an atmosphere of independence, so that at least during that conversation some choices are possible: 'What do you think about . . .' 'Would you like this or that?' are the very basic kind of choices one can offer even when life seems very restricted.

Any conversation with elderly people may include a certain amount of guilt or recrimination about the past. Goodstein suggested that this eased by talking about extenuating circumstances. However, Butler and Lewis (1982, p. 323) take a more robust view.

> Facing genuine guilt as well as the attrition of the person's physical and mental world is what makes psychotherapy with the ageing an intellectually and emotionally powerful experience. The therapist cannot win out against death, but he or she can win out for life, for a sense of the real, for the kind of growth that truly matters, dealing as it does with the evaluation of ways to love and hate, with the meanings of human conduct, an appreciation of human nature, and the succession of the generations.

Butler and Lewis see guilt and atonement as one of the common themes of work with aged people. The need for new starts and second chances, to revitalise, is another. A further theme is that death is around, comes in disguise, that life is not infinite. With that goes an awareness of time leading to simple enjoyment and tranquillity. They identify aspects of grief and restitution, the need to feel secure and confident that all that can be done has been done to recompense for earlier losses, and that one has a safe confidante somewhere in the situation.

There is a strong theme around autonomy and identity, the struggle between being a person knowing who one is, and then being put in a dependent role through some process of infirmity. Helplessness and dependency are very uncomfortable experiences; to alleviate the discomfort they induce some people become dictatorial. Even incontinence can sometimes be viewed as the last weapon of self assertion (Newman, 1978).

Thus there is an existential flavour to psychotherapeutic counselling and some social work activity with vulnerable old people. There is a need for older people to begin to put their lives in order, to review and be helped to see life as a whole, that they have the same 'self over time' (Bakur-Weiner and Taggart White, 1982). This self needs to be encouraged in its self evaluation, in its capacity to enjoy aloneness, as one of the ways through, in the often overwhelming sense of grief and loss which can occur in old age. Reminiscence work, as explored by Coleman (1986) shows a way of consolidating life, by drawing on past experiences to savour them again.

These ideas from psychotherapy help our background understanding of emotional experiences in the later part of the life-cycle.

Conclusion

Despite the rich possibilities of developing social work practice with elderly people and their families, there is caution about suggesting ways of working which are bound to be more time-consuming. The satisfaction offered to elderly clients, and to social workers in working with more understanding of the feelings engaged should not be underestimated.

In establishing a relationship to undertake some form of direct social work, the worker is above all learning to communicate, and to respond accurately to the communications received. These are then assessed, a social care plan formed, and the social work interaction planned and evaluated within a framework. This may be a piece of work offering straightforward short-term helping around obtaining a service. It may be intervention in a crisis, or a task-centred plan sharing the problem-solving activities with the client. At times brief counselling is indicated drawing on insights from psychotherapy. In all these activities the place of the elderly client in the family network should be maintained and enhanced as far as possible. The next chapter will seek to show ways of working with the family as a whole.

5

Working with Families and Carers

Care at home in the community

A vulnerable elderly person is not usually isolated, but is involved with family members, friends and neighbours in a network of relationships, as established in Chapter 1. This chapter in focusing on work with families and carers considers informal care networks and the role of carers, before exploring ways in which social workers can be involved. That may be as part of a multidisciplinary team, or alone, working with the family and family network in a variety of ways. In a survey of community care Griffiths (1988) reported:

> Publicly provided services constitute only a small part of the total care provided to people in need. Families, friends or neighbours and other local people provide the majority of care in response to needs which they are uniquely well placed to identify and respond to. This will continue to be the primary means by which people are enabled to live normal lives in community settings . . . the first task of publicly provided services is to support and where possible strengthen these networks of carers (Griffiths, 1988, p. 5).

He goes on:

> A failure to give proper levels of support to informal carers not only reduces their own quality of life and that of the relative or friend they care for, but is also potentially inefficient as it can lead to less personally appropriate care being offered. Positive action is therefore needed to encourage the delivery of more flexible support which takes account of how best to support and maintain the role of informal carers (Griffiths, 1988, p. 7).

Here, once again, is official recognition of the essential part played by informal care networks in offering independence and a reasonable quality of life to vulnerable elderly people living in a domestic setting. The social work task is to understand the realities of care received and offered within a family network, and to support both the cared for person and the carers. This will involve providing assessment, information, technical know how, services and counselling. It may also involve working with the whole family or family network including all carers, using the techniques of family work used in other social work contexts.

Informal care

Consideration must be given to the distinction between informal and formal care. Informal care is unpaid care; the term, widely used, can seem somewhat derogatory, and caution should be exercised in talking about an informal carer. The term family carer is preferable where appropriate. Formal care is that provided by the mainly statutory services, but also by private agencies. The same person may be a formal carer in paid employment, and a family carer within the family, thus personally carrying a double burden of responsibility.

The nature of caring

The dual nature of the verb to care involving both labour and love shows the essential elements of caring activities (Graham, 1983). All carers whatever their titles or financial status are likely to be engaged in tasks of tending with vulnerable elderly people. This encompasses:

> The actual work of looking after those who temporarily or permanently cannot do so for themselves. It comprises such things as feeding, washing, lifting, cleaning up for the incontinent, protecting, and comforting. It is the more active and face to face manifestation of care (Parker 1981).

This may or may not be accompanied by feelings of affection; the analysis by Graham (1983) that 'Feeling concern and taking charge have both psychological and material connotations' has helped to distinguish these two elements. To keep aware of both doing and feeling helps to clarify in any situation whether the main burden is physical, financial or psychological. Abrams and Marsden (1987) looked at the impact on carers where the tending in some cases was not accompanied by love, and where the length of caring was such that there might be an outworn welcome.

Exploring how nineteen carers, known to a social services support group, experienced the caring relationship, Ungerson (1987, p. 15) focused on:

> the historical biography of the relationship between carer and cared for: how far was it possible for people with a long history on one particular level to relate to each other on a level of physical intimacy, faced with the disgust that caring often demands.

The similarities between caring and mothering, shifting power relationships between mothers and daughters, and issues of 'cross-sex caring' in relation to incest taboos were also areas for exploration in her interviews. This study repays careful reading to understand more of the complexity of domestic care. As she concludes:

> Informal care between family members is very far from being unproblematic; it can and almost always does, raise in an acute form issues of power, bereavement for the loss of a loved personality, anxiety about sole responsibility, and feelings of exploitation and manipulation (ibid.).

Caring can also be viewed as a reciprocal activity over the life course. Three kinds of family obligation have been identified (Finch, 1987c), namely personal care, material or financial assistance of a substantial kind, and the temporary or permanent provision of a home. These obligations may be negotiated on a reciprocal basis over many years, building up a commitment between specific family members (Finch, 1987c). This ties in with Ungerson's consideration of the complex motives of duty. Family property owning patterns are affected by widespread home ownership, so it is not impossible that in addition to ordinary feelings of affection, concern and duty, some carers may be under pressure to care, to save family wealth seeping out in expensive residential care fees.

Who are the carers?

One of the underlying assumptions in our society is that the best most morally valuable care is that provided by family, friends and neighbours. The only snag is: 'Nobody asked if the families wanted to do it, or even could: nobody seriously studied the extent to which there might even be a family' (Whitehorn, 1987).

There seems to be a changing pattern among carers. The great majority of carers were women (EOC, 1980). Allen (1983) found that 85 per cent of carers were women, predominantly daughters, followed by daughters-in-law, other female friends and neighbours. In addition it was established that women tended to receive less support services than male carers (EOC, 1982). It was found that single daughters, as carers, were under greater pressure to give up work or take part-time employment rather than remain in full employment (Wright, 1986).

It has now been shown that the number of male carers has increased substantially. There are 3.5 million women and 2.5 million men caring, with 19 per cent of all households having a dependant in need of care. One factor in this is the number of men taking early retirement or redundancy because there is a dependant in the household (Green, 1988). This pattern is expected to continue into the 1990s. With the overall decline in fertility elderly people have fewer children than in previous generations (Phillipson and Walker, 1986, p. 4), and will be turning to a wider range of friends, relatives and neighbours for help and support. The changing patterns of marriage and companionate relationships will also expand the range of principal carers. When we think and talk about the family we need to think of the household and the significant relationships in a person's life.

The experience of being cared for

To be cared for almost inevitably involves some diminution of independence. It must often seem a 'second best' situation, to be resisted as long as possible, although for some vulnerable people it comes as a relief and a right, after years of effort, to feel someone else is in charge. There is less research into the experience of being cared for. Qureshi and Walker (1986, p. 115) in a survey of people over 75, and their carers found that caring could be a difficult experience for both parties: the lack of alternative resources drove people together, imposing dependency. It has been shown how elderly people move closer to those who can help them sustain their independence, rather than aiming to move in with relatives. People want to sustain a sense of being in control, of still having a contribution to make. In all the difficulties of being cared for, the role of confidante offers one solution. Jerrome (1982) showed how even an annual contact with a real confidante could be wonderfully sustaining.

Taking this further Wenger (1984) was able to show that supportive networks were needed by both sides in the caring relationship; this could be not only the slightly more distant family who by writing, telephoning, and occasional visits kept contact, but also a circle of friends for the carer's own support.

The experience of being a carer

In Chapter 1 attention was drawn to the tangle of relationships within which carers and cared may be enmeshed. The experience of being a personal carer is well researched (Nissel and Bonnerjea, 1982; Levin *et al.*, 1984; Sinclair *et al.*, 1984; Wenger, 1984; Ungerson, 1987; Dalley, 1988). There are also a number of articulate carers, whose visibility is enhanced by the work of the Carers National Association. Broad themes have emerged from these studies which social workers may find helpful to bear in mind. These can be drawn out from within the history of a caring relationship particularly where there is a principal carer taking responsibility.

Motivation   The process of selection by the family, or self selection by the carer, for this work is shown to play a crucial part in the subsequent relationship and caring process. Sometimes a carer is clearly identified by being a spouse, or already resident in the same house. Some relationships drift into dependency and caring without much conscious thought. Families sometimes identify one person as the logical carer, because the person is the oldest, youngest, or has a part-time job. Where the implications of becoming a carer have been discussed in advance by all involved, so that some agreement has been reached about the amount of help it is possible to give, the outlook is more optimistic (Nissel and Bonnerjea, 1982).

Other family members   The composition of the family, both within the household and the extended family, plays a part in the experience of caring, for these people may be supportive and helpful, or indifferent, or hostile. Where a carer feels in conflict with the demands of different people in the household, or even has two dependents, the stress is much greater. If it seems husband or children are paying a high price for the caring in other ways this is difficult. Should the carer feel unsupported personally, or that the cared for person is not valued by other relatives, this again adds to stress.

The role of carer   Caring can involve a variety of roles, not all of which can be comfortably accommodated. To 'mother' a husband, 'parent' a parent, or offer 'professional' nursing care to a spouse may each at times seem abnormal, even though offering the best solution to the circumstances. The case study in Chapter 2 illustrates this.

The biography of the relationship   People enter a caring relationship with the experience of a number of life events in common. The quality of the relationship inevitably affects the caring process. Abrams and Marsden (1987) found that it was easier to care for a heavily dependent person where there was an underlying positive relationship, than to care for a less dependent person where feelings were ambiguous or hostile.

Moral dilemmas are frequently involved in caring. It seems almost impossible to entirely eliminate guilt on either side. These dilemmas involve what is given up or not done in order to care, or prioritisation of need in the family, or the sense of not caring well enough, or not doing enough to help. A particular thorny dilemma arises should the caring situation present demands beyond the level of endurance. At this point permission may need to be sought from trusted advisers or respected family members to consider alternatives. Most carers have attachment and affection to sustain them; recognising that the deepest levels of such feelings are not enough to see the process through, involves some grief. By contrast a strong sense of duty may present a moral dilemma in undertaking caring, for by itself it is a cheerless framework for entering a close and inevitably intimate relationship.

Issues of control   The question 'who is boss?' was identified in the Darlington Community Care project as being particularly difficult to disentangle (Stone, 1987). 'Learned helplessness' can become a powerful weapon, and the pressure of anxious attachment from a vulnerable and very elderly parent can make all separations, however life-saving for the carer, hard to achieve.

Low status of carers Those who give up a job or take early retirement to become a carer lose out financially, and in other ways, as has been well documented (Finch and Groves, 1983). Caring is frequently viewed as a low status activity, imposing a sense of personal responsibility, and possibly a sense of failure subsequently, depending on the circumstances. As part of this process some carers experience that in this capacity, whatever their skills in other directions, they take on the invisibility of their dependent, denigrated in a market oriented society as a burden. Thus it takes considerable courage and persistence at times for the carer to press the needs of the dependent, let alone her/his personal needs.

Carers' own needs It has been identified that people have different capacities to undertake being a carer. One study reports: 'Some women are born carers and copers who take a situation in their stride. Others cannot cope, or cope unsuccessfully: they resent the caring role, or they continually feel guilty or confused' (Nissel and Bonnerjea, 1982). Frequently for a carer, personal needs take second place to the hard physical and mental effort required for the dependant. This entails in a carer's words 'Living someone else's life, thinking for two people'.

It may be too exhausting, painful and risky to consider one's own needs in a situation like being carer, which is not predictable in duration. Yet on a practical level if a carer is to keep going, and to have some life when the caring has ended this personal consideration needs to be encouraged and supported in a variety of ways. Counselling, information and advice giving, respite from caring on a regular basis can all help. Relatives' support groups have such a full agenda that they may become almost swamped by shared suffering unless they have a facilitator who can help ease the 'tension upon tension' one group member described.

Information resources and services

The experience of being a carer is considerably affected by the availability of these facilities. The study of supporters of dementia sufferers (Levin *et al.*, 1984) showed that many were not aware of or not in receipt of home helps, day care, attendance allowance, or social work support. Knowing what is available and what might help is a first step in the process of claiming and receiving such assistance.

Informal care networks

Having explored some aspects of being a principal carer, and the cared for elderly person in a close relationship in a family, we need to look in more detail at the character of informal care networks, where there may be more people involved in a less intense way. Many vulnerable elderly people, particularly those living alone are sustained by a network of friends, neighbours and more distant family calling briefly on a regular or irregular basis.

The Networks Project (Sinclair *et al.*, 1984) helped to clarify how informal care networks function. It looked at formal and informal care for elderly people on their own. Care was identified as being those activities which one person did for another; informal care consisted of practical care, information/advocacy, links with the outside world, regular surveillance, social integration (belonging to a group or having a satisfying role in relation to others) and affection. Sons and daughters could offer the widest variety of support, and were particularly important.

Informal care was seen to be characterised by:

1 *Specialisation*: children, neighbours, friends and other relatives performed different if overlapping roles which could not be fully substituted for each other.
2 *Limitation*: as there were limits to the types and amounts of help the different categories of helpers were expected to provide.
3 *Variability*: as certain clients received more help than others. Some were more able to seek out and use support than others (Sinclair *et al.*, 1984, p. 21).

In this study, carried out in London, one characteristic of the clients was a lack of relatives living close by. A well-supported client was defined as having daily contact with a neighbour and weekly contact with a relative; only one-fifth had this degree of support. On one weekly visit the relative could not cover all the needs of the elderly person. Forty per cent were poorly supported in that they had neither of these contacts at such frequency.

It was significant that loneliness and low morale made clients particularly difficult to support: 'Low social integration and the prospect of residential care decreased morale, while low morale left clients without the heart to play active roles or to fight to stay in their own homes' (Sinclair *et al.*, 1984).

This question of morale is then one of the key areas for social workers to be aware of in sustaining people and their family networks or informal care networks in the community. There is a need to help those who are lonely to feel sufficiently secure in themselves, and sufficiently still a part of life that they want to keep up the struggle to go on coping (see case study 4:1).

Further evidence of the significance of morale, and of the special contribution social workers can make comes through the research conducted by the Personal Social Services Research Unit on domiciliary care, otherwise known as the Kent Community Care Project (Davies and Challis, 1986). They have identified that simply putting in more services may not be in itself sufficient to maintain a situation if motivation is lacking. Most services: 'lack the properties of Heineken lager – they reach only the most obvious parts of the anatomy of need' (Davies and Knapp, 1988, p. 33). The Heineken effect this research has identified is that created by a confiding trusting relationship, which accompanied by appropriate services, achieves more than any other managerial skill they could identify, to encourage elderly people to believe they could manage independent living and avoid admission to residential care. Social workers above all have this capacity to focus on aspects of psychological well-being, and in doing family work to contribute skills in this area to a multidisciplinary team.

A further example of ways to use social work skills in combination with those of other formal carers to maintain informal care networks, has been demonstrated in Darlington (Stone, 1987). This project studied ways to maintain severely disabled people in the community, and out of long stay hospital beds, at less cost than hospital care. The integration of health and social service personnel was an essential part of this scheme. The project manager was a senior social worker and the three service managers all had nursing backgrounds.

Home care aides were selected to work in small teams with the services managers, each having not more than two clients. They combined domestic, personal care, and specialist skills, taught by other professionals, such as physiotherapy, or speech therapy. In-service training, weekly group meetings and monthly supervision sessions were all provided for the home care aides. The service managers also offered support to the family carers.

As a result of this research, some advantages of multidisciplinary working combining skills from different professions would seem to be:

1   The security offered by having service managers with nursing skills particularly when working with severely disabled people.
2   The experience in risk taking which a project manager with a social work background brings.
3   The use of groupwork skills from social work to help in team building work.
4   A management style prepared to pass responsibility down the line.
5   The counselling and family work skills taught through social work leadership to all team members.

This project has been described in some detail for it exemplifies the way social workers may need to adapt their skills, to work with colleagues from other disciplines, and also to work at one remove from the client, in sustaining an informal care network, or a family network.

Social work tasks in family work

It should be clear from consideration of some of the research into caring relationships that sustaining family networks and informal care networks is complex for those who are family members, and for the professionals who are working with the networks on a regular basis. For social workers the task is likely to be primarily to act as co-ordinator of services, but the counselling and supporting role for carer and cared for must not be overlooked.

As indicated, in various parts of the country experimental projects have developed a co-ordinator role, giving it different titles, key worker, case manager, care co-ordinator, nominated social worker. It is clear that the role need not always be undertaken by a social worker, but it also seems clear that in situations of family complexity, or personal loss of morale, social workers have particular skills to offer. Counselling skills were described in chapter 4. We now move on to explore family work skills.

Doing family work

It has now been established that the identified client, the vulnerable elderly person referred to a social service department is most likely to be part of an interlocking network of friends, relatives and neighbours, carers and support services. To help a social worker clear a framework for how to proceed in family work some theoretical ideas may be helpful.

The idea of working with families of elderly people has been more fully explored in American social work texts. Greene (1986) worked out a 'functional age model of intergenerational treatment'. The influences which contributed to the development of this model draw on psycho-analysis, psychosocial casework, ego psychology, role theory, systems theory, family therapy, communication theory and developmental family theory (Greene, 1986, pp. 6–7). This sounds complicated but does give some useful guidelines. The points to be noted are that:

1 The social worker should do a bio-psychosocial assessment taking a careful look at any disruption in the elderly person's capacity to function and to cope, particularly if there has been a health cause to precipitate a referral.
2 The focus of the social worker is on the 'client system', which may either be a tight knit family system, or a more loosely structured family network, or an informal care network.
3 The social worker should proceed to explore the organisation and structure of the family system, the roles people play within it, and the way the changes in the old person have affected that.
4 The developmental stage of the family as a whole should be considered, and what other life crises the family are facing, for example retirement of carers, marriage of grandchildren, death of other relatives.

In approaching family work in this way a social worker may want to arrange for a multidisciplinary assessment, calling on advice from the health care team. It will be important to take a biographical view of the build-up of the caring network. As well as working with the elderly person, it will be important to work with family members, so that the impact of recent changes is recognised throughout the family system, and all are engaged in working together towards accommodating those changes and losses. The social worker may be able to free up some complex feelings; however the emphasis in this kind of work is on the impact of recent events, not on trying to unscramble past jealousies and conflicts.

The work will normally be with an elderly person's family, the children, and grandchildren, but the family of origin may be valuable if there are siblings still available, near at hand. For childless elderly people in particular these brothers or sisters may provide a strong support.

In moving into family work the social worker has a complex number of responsibilities to balance:

1   The interests of the elderly person and the rest of the family network, which may sometimes be in competition.
2   The agency responsibility to ensure fair distribution of services.
3   The guardianship of those resources.

The Wagner report (1988) recognised that this role conflict could be paralysing at times and suggested that social workers should be clear which role has priority at any one time.

In working with a family, after an initial assessment interview primarily with the elderly person, the social worker may find him/herself working with:

1   A dyad, that is marital interaction, domestic partnership, parent/child, landlady/lodger.
2   A tryad, or family system.
3   A family network.

These different kinds of interaction will be discussed in turn.

Dyadic relationships

Marital interaction

Later-life marriages are often relationships which contain within them intense feelings, whether of warmth, companionship and expression of sexuality, or of ambivalence contained for years (Hemmings, 1985). Even a kind of guerrilla warfare is enjoyed and can in itself be life sustaining (Mattinson and Sinclair, 1979). Elderly couples continue to have a number of adjustments to make, getting used to different patterns of daily living, changing forms of sexual expression, failing health and senses, shifting roles. Social workers could help to assist communication patterns, or to enable partners to feel close, but without their individuality swamped by the changing needs of the other.

It is difficult within organisational constraints for social workers to find the time to do marital work and it is even harder to find time to do so for elderly couples. Social workers who want to give serious attention to an elderly couples' relationship which is causing unhappiness might find it helpful to find a colleague with whom to talk through their feelings about doing marital work, including the discussion of sexuality with an elderly couple. The worker's personal feelings may need to be acknowledged first, before it is possible to embark on the kind of work in which a couple of the generation of the worker's parents or grandparents are encouraged to express their sexuality and personal needs.

Domestic partnerships

Revealing the painful side of the very private area of a marriage or close domestic partnership involves breaking social taboos, and sympathetic response to the first hint of difficulty helps the communication (Wilson and James, 1987).

The variety of close relationships with which people end their lives should be acknowledged. Gay or lesbian relationships, the latter described movingly by Macdonald and Rich (1984), should be recognised. The companionate relationships of convenience may be different. Not all will have a sexual component. In contrast the relationships of landlady and lodger, landlord and tenant may have this component. The important factor to recognise is the meaning which attaches to the relationship for both parties, and how the pair can accommodate the changing functional capacity of one or both of them.

Impact of illness on a relationship

So often the strength and meaning of a partnership is only revealed when one person is gravely ill or dies.

For example, Mrs Y. was a nervous anxious woman, whose husband had a cerebral haemorrhage, resulting in a stroke which particularly affected his arm and his speech. Without his reassurance Mrs Y. lost her confidence and her grip on life; she was unable to function, so that neither could cope. First he was admitted to a Part III residential home, and then she was admitted with him. The daughter called on the social worker to assist because without speech there were general communication problems. The speech therapist confirmed that Mr Y. had only limited understanding of what was happening to him. Here is an example of a need for multidisciplinary work, in which the social worker lacked the expert knowledge needed to handle the case alone. The interaction between husband and wife was knocked off balance by a particular type of illness which resulted in a role reversal; the stronger and more dominant partner became weak. The work needed to be co-ordinated by the social worker, with rehabilitation specialists, to assist the couple as a system to cope with the change in their previous patterns of interaction.

Family meetings

Family meetings are increasingly being used in childcare work, with mentally handicapped clients, and with adolescents (Gorell Barnes, 1984). So far relatively little has been written about the use of review meetings or family meetings in work with elderly people, although their value in practice is increasingly being recognised. It is not really a family meeting unless the old person concerned is present. The following two case studies show the kind of situation where a family meeting is a helpful part of the social work plan. First, a complex case involved an old lady with mental illness and her abused daughter. This piece of work demanded a bio-psychosocial approach and social care planning finally culminating in a family meeting.

Case studies

An 83 year-old woman insisted that her 59 year-old daughter and son-in-law aged 60, continue to live with her in her council flat after their relatively recent marriage. Mrs R. was referred by her general practitioner to the social services office for assessment. On the first visit the social worker met the son-in-law as she arrived, rushing out of the flat, with the door slammed. She found the daughter in tears in the kitchen, refusing to speak. The old lady was not mentally impaired on first impression. The social worker did not get very far, but having decided to leave, met the son-in-law returning, outside the flat. He said that his mother-in-law was dementing, on top of being a 'nasty woman'. She ruled their lives with a rod of iron, would not let TV be on after 10 p.m., cancelled the daily papers, and insisted that her daughter continue to share her bedroom, while he slept alone in the spare room. Mrs R. was a heavy smoker, and this was a fire hazard. She pinched bruises on her daughter's inner arm, and had poured hot tea on both daughters. She was the tenant of the flat and did not want to move so the daughter and her husband had no rights to that accommodation.

In assessing the situation, and planning her interaction, the social worker aimed first to get Mrs R. to modify her behaviour, without success. The next move in social care planning was to advise the daughter and son-in-law to leave, applying to be rehoused. This 'shocking' suggestion was eventually accepted, with the promise of back-up facilities for Mrs R. A council flat was allocated within two weeks. When they moved our Mrs R. would only let them take a bed and some crockery.

In view of the fact that this old woman was at risk of starting a fire and had never lived alone, the social worker obtained support from all the services on a programme of observation and assessment in the house, for four days, with a back-up place in a home. A night sitter was booked for the first night, with a home care aide to go in several times the following day. The night sitter left at 7 a.m. and the home care aide was due to come at 8 a.m. Mrs R. knocked on the neighbour's door at 7.30 a.m. and the police were called. By 2 p.m. that day she was in a very anxious state and accepted the social worker's offer of a short stay bed on a trial basis to help her make a decision. The staff of the Home were involved, and Mrs R. opted for a permanent place and was transferred at once.

By this time Mrs R. was not speaking to her daughter so the social worker aimed to improve this relationship. She accompanied the daughter three times on visits to help break the tension. Then after ten weeks in residential care a *family meeting* was planned.

Mrs R., both daughters, the key worker in the Home, and the social worker were present. There was a certain amount of anxiety lest Mrs R. decide she wanted to go home again, but she did not. By this time she was more relaxed and less frightened. She agreed to give up her home and some furniture was brought for her present accommodation. She was then able to spend occasional weekends at her daughters' flats, but still gave the residential staff a hard time on her return.

The social workers commented that in this very 'stuck' situation something had to give to get any movement; it was necessary to encourage the daughter to take the independence she should have had many years ago. It shows good practice that the social worker did not withdraw once the immediate situation was resolved by admission to Part III, but continued to work for reconciliation, and to lessen guilt, so that all feelings were beginning to be worked through. This meant there was less likely to be a change of mind from the old lady or daughter. Additional difficulties in this piece of work lay in distinguishing if there was brain failure, a part of the dementing process, or a life-long pattern of domineering behaviour within the household accompanied by short term memory lapses. The amount of time that needed to be spent in co-ordinating services, and in involving the residential care staff fully at each stage, was considerable, but this resulted in their incorporation in the family network, and rightful attendance at a family meeting.

CASE STUDY 5.3 – MRS J.

In this second case a family meeting was used to help a family give an uncomfortable message. This involved a woman aged 92, and her four sons aged 54, 63, 68, and 72. Mrs J. was referred by the GP for respite care. The background indicated that previously she had lived with her youngest son for seven years; over time, arguments developed with the daughter-in-law. Mrs J. was a dominant person, so much so that she ended up in hospital suffering from malnutrition, as she had refused to eat. When she was ready for discharge the youngest son said he could not take her back. The second youngest, who was remarried one year before, offered her a place in his bungalow. He found that Mrs J., being such a strong-willed person, was difficult to live with, and was incontinent, so relief was needed. Just after the GP had made the request for respite care this daughter-in-law suddenly died. Immediate care was then needed for Mrs J.

When the social worker first interviewed Mrs J. she presented as a tall active upright person, totally deaf, who railed about her dead daughter-in-law, to the great distress of the son. An emergency admission to Part III was arranged, and a review fixed for six weeks after admission. The daughters-in-law made it clear that Mrs J. had given all of them a hard time over the years. The social worker explored with Mrs J. the fact that she could not live with any of them again. She refused to believe this and always said: 'Terry, (or John, or Derek) will have me; I shan't settle otherwise'. The social worker decided that the only way forward was a *family meeting* as the sons individually could not tell their mother the situation. Sons and spouses attended the meeting, having prepared beforehand that they would tell their mother personally that they could not offer her a home, but would keep in touch with her, and support her with regular visits. The social worker was present throughout this meeting in which Mrs J. was naturally very upset. Arrangements were made for her to go to a home specialising in care for people who were motivated to look after themselves, and the staff were prepared to cope with the deafness. She has now settled in; she is doing more for herself, and sometimes she is full of life in the Home.

In this situation the social worker planned to offer the family time and encouragement, to help them realise that if uncomfortable messages are not delivered, it breeds even more resentment and antagonism; intolerable situations build up. The way through was by a supported family meeting.

These examples from practice show how family work offers a way to get even uncomfortable messages across, because the family as a whole is taking responsibility with the elderly person for major life transitions. This is evidence of continuing support from the family in weathering the changes.

So often with old people it is the death of a relative or principal carer or change of residence or even both, which provokes a crisis. The examples also demonstrate the complexity of the family situations which are referred to social workers; if a situation can be resolved by commonsense solutions, and talking through with friends and relatives, then this is usually achieved privately. Only those situations which are really knotted, with personality or relationship difficulties of long standing, tend to come the way of a qualified or specialist social worker for elderly people.

Meetings to maintain a family network

Social service practice

Family network meetings to help maintain the web of relationships sustaining a vulnerable elderly client have been used in Social Service practice (Rawlings, 1988). Building on current practice in case conferences it was found that one difference was that a network meeting involved the client and unpaid informal or family carers, as well as representatives from statutory and voluntary agencies as appropriate. The meeting aimed to help the client make choices and take risks, and to be more in control of their own lives.

Another advantage is that the open nature of the meeting means that it is less easy to split workers and carers.

Rawlings worked out a procedure for network meetings similar to that used in a child abuse case conference. The duties of the person chairing it include:

(a) To perform introductions.
(b) To give everyone present the opportunity of contributing information and of saying what they or their agency could offer.
(c) To arbitrate and try to think about the situation in terms of all the agencies present.
(d) To control discussions, keeping them relevant.
(e) To pull theories together, towards making a decision and a treatment plan.

(f) To help clear anxiety and to get it into the open, to put on record and share responsibility.

(g) To explain the law where necessary, and explain jargon (Rawlings, 1988).

Problems of confidentiality may arise if the client does not want everyone present to hear all that is discussed. There are problems of recording and circulating minutes. Thus many of the issues that arise over open case conferences with client access also occur in network meetings. The introduction of informal carers, and other interested parties, for example a landlord, creates problems which have to be thought through beforehand.

Thorough preparation ensures the success of the network meeting, with the likelihood that the social worker as key worker/case manager/nominated social worker has a simpler task thereafter. The network functions more smoothly with better internal communication.

Family network meetings: brief problem-focused intervention – a Health Authority approach

Pottle (1984) described family work as part of a preventive approach with mentally infirm people, which demonstrates the broader view of a network as relevant to an elderly person's situation. The team involved a psychiatrist, community psychiatric nurse and social worker and used a family or network meeting of brief problem-focused intervention. This had to involve the person who most wanted the situation to change, as well as the elderly person and other relevant people. The usual questions were raised at the meeting;

What is the problem?
To whom is it a problem?
How is it a problem to them?
What are the solutions so far?
How can the team help?

They planned each meeting to last an hour normally, and having gathered the information the team withdrew separately to ask themselves 'Why is this a problem now?' The solution suggested often involved a positive reframing of all the good work currently being done by the family, neighbours, and home help, and the wish of the old person to retain independence. In discussion in one case, for example, it was accepted that an old couple with very high standards were unlikely to want anyone else cleaning the house. This allowed the wife space to say she urgently needed help, and gave the husband more time to think it over, knowing how she felt. One of the purposes of network meetings is to negotiate emotional space for people to face up to hard decisions, and to show the reality of the way the current situation looks to all involved.

Family therapy

Family therapy is a field of practice mainly built around and developed from systems theory. Social workers play a part with other professionals, notably psychologists and psychiatrists in a family therapy team, often working with younger families from a clinical setting. Workers offer co-therapists to work with a family, or work as a family team. The main approaches include the psychoanalytic (Waldrond-Skinner, 1976), structural (Minuchin, 1981), and strategic/systemic (Palazzoli *et al.*, 1980); each have their specific techniques and theoretical formulations. Many social workers will already be familiar with these ideas from their work with younger families (Gorell Barnes, 1984; Coulshed, 1988).

A relative dearth of literature and experience unfortunately hampers the development of family therapy with older families particularly in the United Kingdom, with a few notable exceptions. (Lieberman, 1979; Pincus, 1981; Sher, 1983; Evans, 1985; Quigley and Womphrey, 1988). This reflects many of the factors already discussed about the development of social work practice with old people. More particularly family therapy requires a commitment of time and effort from all the participants, with a hope of long-term gain.

However, if we acknowledge that family communications follow a pattern developed over time, and this can be usefully observed and adapted with younger families, is it not reasonable to assume that with older families too such a process could be helpful in some cases? The insights from family therapy which can be helpful have been identified (Bogo, 1987). Building on the recognition that families have repetitive patterns of behaviour it is suggested that a social worker joins a family group, by listening to each individual in turn. It might then be possible to begin to analyse the boundaries, alignments and the power in the family drawing on the work of Minuchin (1981).

One might establish the nature of the boundaries within the family. Very diffuse boundaries between its members indicate an enmeshed family who may be over involved; very rigid boundaries, with minimal involvement are a sign of the disengaged family. It is more likely that a family will lie somewhere on the continuum between these positions in its behaviour patterns. The concept of alignment recognises how one member of a family system may oppose or join with another in carrying out some task. As an elderly member deteriorates in health the patterns of alliance may shift. This concept is also linked with the concept of power, which is one used to indicate how much influence a family member has in achieving a desired outcome, by active or passive alignment with other members.

An elderly person in weakening health may be able to exert more power in the family and even to prevail on a disengaged family member to play a more active part in discussion and in regular visiting (Bogo, 1987).

An example of the strategic approach of reframing (Palazzoli *et al.*, 1980) has already been described in the family network meeting (Pottle, 1984).

Insights from family therapy can be quite widely applied to help social workers understand the family process. The next step is to offer additional techniques to give a family space to explore the way the patterns of past relationships affect the problems, and decisions made in the present.

For example the use of family therapy in helping to disentangle one or two cases of elder abuse have been described (Quigley and Womphrey, 1988). In one case a contract was agreed and several sessions were held with a family consisting of grandmother, her son and his wife and their three teenage children. These sessions were held to explore why the family were unable to let go the mentally infirm grandmother, who had already been abused. Permanent care had been offered and refused. Factors which emerged related to the dependent relationship between the father and his elderly mother, and to the long-standing unsatisfactory state of the couple's marriage.

The family kept together by focusing on the daily difficulties of life with the grandmother.

A creative approach to the use of family therapy techniques with later life families is to be encouraged. A support group of workers all interested in breaking new ground might be set up. With increasing longevity more families will become four and five generation ones, often influenced emotionally by some very elderly relative, so that development of this area of therapy is bound to be fruitful. Where young people are receiving family therapy, their grandparents and great-grandparents should be included more frequently in the family meeting, acknowledging that later life is still an essential part of family life.

Conclusion

The purpose of this chapter has been to show how carers and the informal care network becomes part of the family network, and possibly even part of the family system with which social workers must work. This involves understanding the perspective of the elderly client, of the carers and how the caring relationship developed. Network meetings provide an opportunity and a space, facilitated by the social worker and other professionals, in which concerns surrounding continuing care in the community for a particular person can be voiced and talked through.

In the past review meetings have sometimes been held in the absence of the elderly client. Now we need to develop the good practice of making sure that the client is there, to give rights and responsibilities back to vulnerable elderly clients within their family situation. It helps to make it possible for people to face openly the ambivalence of the caring relationship on both sides, with the possibility of conflict where it exists. Family work with elderly people is a very skilled activity.

The next chapter explores social work practice where a family member begins to need residential care.

6

Group Care in Residential Care Homes

Up to now the emphasis in this book has been on demonstrating ways in which social workers can help maintain a vulnerable elderly person in the community, by working with the client and family network. In many cases this care can continue with adjustments in the amount of support until the elderly person dies. Residential care has been viewed and therefore avoided as something of a last resort. This may be in part a legacy from the old workhouse image which still persists (Sinclair, 1988b, p. 279).

In this chapter I hope to explore family work in the context of the admission to a residential home of a family member. I want to point up examples of good practice which will enable a vulnerable elderly person to transfer into the group care setting, keeping a sense of identity and a family network intact, with the possibility that residential staff become part of the extended family network, or social support system. Much of what is said can also be applied to a day care setting.

To do this the focus will be on the following areas:

1 Social work with residential homes.
2 The transition to group care.
3 The needs of an elderly person in a residential home.
4 Work with the family network.
5 Issues around private residential care.
6 The roles of the social worker.

Working with staff in residential care homes

The definition of a residential care home in the Registered Homes Act 1984 is:

Any establishment which provides or is intended to provide, whether for reward or not, residential accommodation with both board and personal care, for four or more persons in need of personal care by reasons of old age, disablement, past or present dependence on alcohol or drugs or past or present mental disorder.

This Act referred primarily to private establishments but the same criteria should be applied to local authority homes. The important distinction between accommodation and services, recognised in the Wagner report (1988) helps us to focus on the fact that a complete environment is being offered.

A person admitted to a residential home is joining a different social system, away from the family. Yet it is possible, assisted by a social worker or other knowledgeable outsider, to help integrate the family of the new resident into the system of the home. To do this it helps to understand something of the background of residential care, and how issues around gender, dependency, daily routine, and staff responsibility impinge on the environment.

The background to residential care

Since the National Assistance Act 1948 replaced the Poor Law institutions with local authority residential homes, there have been changes of emphasis. It was at first hoped to offer hotel type accommodation which residents chose, as a third option to hospital or community care. The poverty of many applicants, pressure to clear hospital beds, and the cost of the provision of good quality residential care led to a change in priorities away from 'choice' to 'needs' (Sinclair, 1988b). Local authorities did buy in places in voluntary and private Homes occasionally to meet the needs of clients referred to them, but this declined by 1980. Pressure was put on residents to make increasing use of a discretionary power to pay board and lodging through the supplementary benefit supplied by the Department of Health and Social Security. The extension of this power in 1983 to cover elderly people in residential care and nursing homes led to the growth in the number of private home places, which more than doubled from 1979–84, and was estimated to be continuing to rise (Audit Commission, 1986). The mounting costs of these supplementary benefit payments from central government unbalanced both the residential care scene and that of community care. Efforts to change the situation were recommended (Audit Commission, 1986; Griffiths, 1988; Wagner, 1988).

Social workers were reluctant to become involved in negotiations with private facilities, but the state funding for so many elderly people in private Homes has led to an inextricable mix up between the private, voluntary and statutory sectors. Social workers may be asked in future to undertake a functional and financial assessment before state funds can subsidise an elderly person in a private rest home. If such people are to receive advice in making their own choices, social workers are likely to have to continue their involvement with all these parts of the welfare economy. A section of this chapter will explore some of the particular issues raised by working with private homes.

On admission a person tends to lose an individual identity. The needs of the organisation become paramount. There is a basic conflict between the medical model of care and a social work model (Willcocks, 1986). A social work model of care helps to retain identity, but unfortunately many homes adopt a more medical approach, particularly some in the private sector where the proprietors have a nursing qualification. A medical model has a strict routine, whereas a social work model allows for more individual autonomy and choice in matters such as times of getting up, going to bed, and going out for independent activities, which might conflict with staff shifts and rotas.

Gender issues

It is sometimes hard to recognise how much issues of gender are embedded into residential care. Although many homes may be managed by men, most of the low paid care assistants, and many of the residents are likely to be women. Gender difference indicates that people will be admitted to care at a point when for older women they are likely to be frail and dependent, whereas men are admitted earlier when they are fitter, and may live longer in a home, settling more comfortably (Willcocks, 1986, p. 151). Women outnumber men by three to one in residential care. This fact may to some extent explain the low standards of care and privacy sometimes experienced. It has been suggested that degradation on the inside reflects beliefs about the role of women and the rights of elderly women in particular, an example of sexism and ageism in practice (Phillipson, 1981, p. 198). Women are likely to experience residential care in a qualitatively different way to men. Women may suffer that added denigration of being a carer who can no longer care (Evers, 1981).

Care staff experience other pressures. Some may choose to work with vulnerable elderly people out of altruism, and a genuine desire to work with this age group. Others may find the part time or flexible hours the main incentive, or be at the beginning or end of a working life. Most staff are untrained and there is as yet little evidence that training makes much difference to the quality of care (Sinclair, 1988b, p. 270). Thus we have low status, low paid women care assistants, given little overt recognition for the demanding and difficult task they do, caring mostly for elderly women. To this one might add the comment that racism can compound the difficulties where Afro-Caribbean or Asian care assistants receive racist comments in their work from residents (Norman, 1987b).

Dependency

The dependency levels of residents can profoundly affect the environment in residential care. One concern is that as the numbers of very aged people increase in the population, so those offered a place in a home are increasingly dependent. A major longitudinal study followed up residents in 175 homes for elderly people and found no evidence of continuing upward trends in overall levels of dependency (Booth *et al.*, 1982). The number of severely dependent people newly admitted had fallen by the end of the study. While there were fluctuations, it seemed officers in charge did not draw attention to the periods when dependency levels were lighter. Newly admitted residents tended to be more active at the point of admission, having replaced a heavily dependent person.

Daily life

The regime in many residential care homes lacks variety and has been well documented. The common threads of activity and inactivity have been graphically noted by the *Time for Action* study

(Godlove *et al.*, 1982). Observations were noted at ten second intervals for a number of old people in four different settings, day centres, day hospitals, geriatric hospital wards and local authority residential homes. Their conclusions:

> We probably spent more time watching what happens in facilities where care is provided for the elderly than anyone has done before. The data we collected leads inescapably to the conclusion that for most of the time nothing happens at all – this seems to be particularly the case in residential settings (ibid., p. 58).

Staff were noted to spend a minimum of interaction time with residents, sometimes as little as three minutes in a six hour period. Even if someone is physically able to get to and from the toilet and meals unaided, this still allows no time for social care.

The same dilemma occurs in private homes (Weaver *et al.* 1985, p. 139). Social care in a group care setting covers the time spent talking with and listening to people, hearing their stories, nurturing and encouraging them in the effort to make sense of the later stages of life. This work is emotionally costly, as it is often painful to watch the struggle to maintain independence and a sense of self-worth. Training, support and supervision would surely help in this aspect of the work.

Staff responsibility

A heavy responsibility is placed on staff in a home offering twenty-four hour care. This tertiary level of care is the most highly skilled and complex to provide; residents are very vulnerable when so much of their daily lives is out of their hands (Richards, M. 1987, p. 8). The task is how to provide the kind of help which maintains a person's sense of identity and least damages the recipient's self esteem (ibid). A group of residents in an old peoples' home may between them be confronting many occasions of loss and death; the handling of these matters requires sensitivity too.

The Wagner Report set the goal that residential care should offer a positive experience: 'actively aimed at providing every resident with the highest quality of life of which they are capable and indeed a better life than would be open to them in any other environment' (ibid., p. 8).

Social workers can help by understanding the demanding nature of residential care, and by building bridges in ways that will be explained.

The transition to group care

The decision to apply for a place in a residential care home is very often a traumatic one, whether it is a planned or an emergency admission.

Emergency admissions

Admissions do not always take place in ideal circumstances, especially where a crisis has arisen. Some local authorities keep temporary beds for assessment purposes to forestall permanent admissions arising out of crises; this allows for reflection and mobilisation of other services. A crisis tends to arise out of a deterioration in health, or even the death of a carer, spouse or relative.

> A 'plea for removal' crisis is one in which family members or neighbours or relatives or other professional agents and agencies such as . . . police, GPs, health visitors and district nurses, plead for or urgently request, the removal of the individual at the centre of the crisis (O'Hagan, 1986, p. 40).

A great deal of pressure is then put on the social worker to act in the way the majority want, and not spend time listening to what the client wants. O'Hagan suggested it was important to try to prevent the client seeing the social worker as just one more person determined to take him/her away from home regardless of the feelings.

Emergency admissions develop a momentum of their own, not least because in some areas it seems the only way to get a place in a local authority residential home (Sinclair, 1988b). Thus a certain brinkmanship has gone on, with a hospital discharging an elderly person home, ostensibly on trial and then refusing to re-admit when in two or three days it is clear the person cannot cope. One example of bad practice of this kind occurred where a hospital refused to re-admit a patient three days after discharge, and the senior social worker in desperation on a Friday afternoon sent a taxi driver to pick up a vulnerable old woman, to gather together her things, and take her into a residential care home. The [student] social worker was not available that day, and the indications were that the client could not last the weekend. Here a breakdown in communication and planning between hospital and area team demonstrates how pressures pile up, leaving a vulnerable person totally powerless, and deprived of any control of what was happening. Better practice would have been to discharge such a patient on a Monday and monitor her progress daily, to forestall a weekend crisis.

Given that such an emergency admission should be avoided at all costs, how can a social worker plan an admission so that it offers the person concerned a positive choice?

Planned admissions

The first approach for the social worker should be to recognise that the discussions with the client and the family network are beginning to point to residential care as a positive possible option. Families are almost bound to be aware of the slippage in faculties or capacity to cope of an older family member, long before there is an expressed need for some form of group care, whether day care or residential care. This recognition is one of several premonitions of loss which accompany the ageing of parents for adult children, and the elderly person concerned.

In a study of potential nursing home residents it was observed that the old people were likely to undergo a major psychological upheaval as they realised that they must soon give up their own homes and accept institutionalisation for the rest of their lives (Tobin and Lieberman, 1976). This study showed that the anticipation and the worry had as much effect as the actual admission procedure. There are the expected losses of leaving a home, possessions, friends and neighbourhood. There is the deeper psychic fear of separation and of being abandoned to the care of strangers, which reactivates old childhood insecurities and anxieties.

To assist with these feelings, great care should be taken to help the person feel in charge of this process of admission, taking a step which feels right at this time. Social workers really do need to take a stand alongside the old person involved listening and respecting the expressed wishes as far as possible. It is noteworthy that old people may not always have a sense of choice about whether or not to go into residential care. It has been found that it was rare that an old person initiated a request for admission to a local authority home (Stapleton, 1979; Sinclair, 1988b). Within private care where the element of choice might have been thought to be an advantage it was found that a third of residents did not choose, and for 22 per cent the unsolicited efforts of either a relative, the general practitioner or a social worker led to their admission (Weaver *et al.*, 1985).

Many old people face up to accepting the necessity for admission to a residential home, on the basis of discussion within the family and advice from professional workers. The balance between protection and risk taking is always a hard one to get right. If the risks of allowing a person to remain at home seem too great the views of neighbours and family must be given weight, as in the case of the blind woman described in Chapter 2.

The emotional preparatory work, talking through some of these feelings, can take some time to achieve and is as well started before a formal request for admission is completed. The organisational complexities of allocating vacancies in local authority homes will differ in each area, but are designed to minimise conflict within the organisation rather than to meet the needs of individuals, where there is competition for places. When and where a vacancy is offered depends as much on other applicants, the number of vacancies, and the pressures within any given home, as on the wishes, needs and timing for the client in question.

Once a vacancy has been offered, in authorities where there are guidelines for good practice, the social worker should have at least two weeks to make use of the vacancy for the client. This allows time for an introductory visit, alone or with relatives. Sometimes the officer in charge is able to visit the client at home or in hospital. This period allows space for choosing what piece of furniture, ornaments, books and clothes to take, and to find homes for pets and other treasured possessions. Two weeks is not a long time especially as social workers have many competing claims on their time. Hence the value of early preparation.

Family members too will have considerable feelings, and this might be an opportunity for a family meeting in the old person's home, acknowledging the sadness for everybody of having to give up that home, accepting the necessity for more care, and with it the reassurance that the family will be vitally needed for continued regular visiting and involvement. A social worker could facilitate that kind of meeting, making it safe for painful things to be said, past help acknowledged.

Each old person admitted to residential care should sign a contract relating to the rights of residents for accommodation services and continuing personal independence (Wagner, 1988, p. 37). A more explicit example of a contract suggests that it should contain three elements:

1   The rights and responsibilities of the resident.
2   A statement of how residents can be involved in decision-making on how the home is run.
3   An individual care plan for the resident (Corden and Preston-Shoot, 1987, pp. 65–69).

The needs of residents and families

In considering the lives of old people in residential homes, the hierarchy of needs described by Maslow (1970) is useful. In a strange environment peoples' basic needs become even more important. These are for physical warmth, food, clothing and cleanliness. Next in order of necessity are the safety needs, for physical and emotional safety. Physical safety might include not being allowed to wander into dangerous surroundings, or to bathe in scalding hot water. Emotional safety includes the sense of security that comes from being treated with kindness and consistency, not being shouted at. Then the needs for affection and a sense of belonging can be fulfilled. The highest levels of self-esteem and of self-actualisation may be met less frequently in a residential home but should still be aimed for.

Yet for many old people the meeting of basic needs in residential care is problematic. This was revealed in a survey carried out by Kelly (1987) for the Wagner committee. He analysed more than 100 responses to a television programme *Help* asking for experiences of residential care. Forty-six per cent were in favour, 46 per cent against residential homes, with 6 per cent making both positive and negative comments. Fifty-six per cent of respondents were relatives and friends, 30 per cent were residents, 13 per cent were staff. The characteristics described were almost entirely physical showing where the basic anxieties lie. However, assuming that basic needs have been met, self-esteem and self-actualisation can be assisted by allowing some measure of independence, and some place for family members to contribute.

Independence

To ensure a good quality of life elderly people in residential care continue to need the opportunity to exercise autonomy, independence and choice in some areas. Standards vary in how much choice is offered in daily life. The code of practice for private homes *Home Life* (Avebury, 1984) has outlined a level of good practice not yet attained in all local authority homes, particularly in matters such as consultation with residents, consideration of their dignity and respect for personal privacy. For example Camden social services department made public the findings of an independent review of their homes which revealed that lack of recreational activities and opportunities for choice, lack of training for staff and management difficulties were all interwoven (Booth, 1987). More positively Sinclair (1988b, p. 266) has emphasised: 'Residents are adult and most are lucid. Their expressions of what they want and need should be taken seriously.'

The areas in which choice is wanted may be relatively simple to offer. They want to be in control of certain ordinary aspects of life, like opening a window, turning off a radiator, being able to return to a bedsitter at intervals during the day, and to be private or quiet. Security of stay is one aspect which may not be guaranteed. The threat of removal elsewhere, if one's condition gets worse, is one that hangs over the heads of vulnerable elderly people in both private and local authority residential homes in many cases. Residents will not always want the same thing. For some a very routine existence would be a first choice.

Staff need support in the area of risk taking, to allow residents to retain some capacities for self-care and some independence.

If residents are to make choices, these will include going shopping, out to a centre of worship, staying up late, or getting up late. In one home a somewhat unhappy new resident was allowed to spend the first week after admission dressed in her coat and sleeping in a chair. 'It's her home, she must settle in when she's ready', was the attitude of the officer in charge. In these examples we can see the conflict between keeping an establishment on the medical model, and offering something approaching a real home.

Tobin and Lieberman (1976) found that passivity was an indicator that a person was likely to respond badly to being in an institution. They also identified that more passive people were likely to accept the idea of residential care so that homes are more likely to have as residents the 'passive responders' rather than the 'active initiators' identified by Evers (1981) in her study of a long-stay hospital ward. Old people may adopt a passive stance trying to control the anger about being forced to seek admission in order not to upset the equilibrium in the family and not to antagonise the staff looking after them. Self-survival skills become paramount and evident in so many ways, as described by Newton (1980). This Australian woman was admitted to a nursing home by her relatives because of a heart condition, but managed to keep a journal, and organise her life afresh to move out to her own flat, before writing about life on the inside.

Needs of families

There is more widespread acceptance of the use of institutions in the later stages of life in the USA, Canada and Australia, and a considerable body of literature of the ways in which social workers can assist families and their elders to cope with the experience.

Solomon (1982) described four crises facing families around the institutionalisation of an elderly relative. These are the decision to enter, the actual admission, the move to more intensive care, and death. It is to be hoped that the staff of the residential establishment concerned will help families work through their feelings at all these stages.

Whenever an elderly family member is admitted there is likely to be some anxiety for all involved. The old person may fear being cut off, and the family may feel they are abdicating responsibility, experiencing some guilt. Whether an old person is contributing part or all of the financial costs, in a private, voluntary or local authority home, the emotional feelings are likely to be similar. Families do need to be welcomed into the life of the home, to have easy access, and some privacy to talk to their relative. An old person is helped to retain a sense of individuality through maintaining close relationships. Relatives can be comforted in the shock of admission that their job is far from over. The strain of caring physically for someone may be lifted, but the emotional responsibility is not. Families can be encouraged to take the relative out for the day for as long as that can be managed, and to carry on visiting at least weekly. All the tasks such as keeping in touch with old friends, seeing to clothes, financial affairs, and dealing with problems within the home can be carried out by family members.

Relationships between staff and family are not always easy and indeed may seem to become competitive. Resentment from staff that families are not caring for their own, and guilt from relatives at not being able to do so can make communication awkward (Clough, 1981). The social work role in relation to the families of residents is considered at the end of this chapter.

Provision for particular needs

Booth (1985) identified that there are likely to be multiple regimes in local authority homes, with very frail residents likely to be more bound by regulations than more active alert people. I would like to extend this idea and suggest that in larger homes there are likely to be groups of residents with particular needs requiring appropriate provision, such as those with severe physical disability, considerable mental infirmity, ethnic minority elders more estranged than usual in a residential environment, and those who are terminally ill or dying.

Severe physical disability It is always problematic for a residential home to accommodate too many severely disabled people. The number of wheel chairs that can be fitted in, and the number of residents needing regular help with toileting, washing and dressing, has to be balanced alongside the needs of other residents. This issue has been raised in the earlier section on dependency. Much depends on having a good provision of aids geared to the needs of those in residence, not 'hand me downs' from previous occupants, to maximise individual independence.

Mental infirmity Some of the issues around mental infirmity have been unpacked in Chapter 3, but certain aspects need further exploration when thinking of life in a residential setting. Residents with some degree of mental impairment are likely to form a high proportion of those in a residential home, given that most old people in care are over eighty, and one in five of those over eighty are likely to suffer from dementia (Norman, 1987a). The label 'confusion' masks a number of causes, as explained earlier, including depression, infectious diseases, unhappiness or misery, as well as deterioration of brain tissue, as in Alzheimer's disease, or multi-infarct dementia.

Mental impairment demonstrates itself in loss of memory for recent events, and in behavioural, cognitive and emotional change, so that the previous personality is gradually eroded. This 'living death' of a loved person is one of the hardest aspects for carers to cope with. There are recognisable stages which it is helpful to know about. (Marshall (1988, p. 7) explained how memory loss affects completion of tasks, forgetting what one was asked to do, or where one was. Poor judgement is a result, not least over money matters, problems finding words, reading, writing and numbers, and problems with dressing and personal care, requiring personal supervision. The loss of spontaneity and initiative may be accompanied by personality changes, anxiety and restlessness, particularly around tea time.

Gradually weight loss occurs despite a good diet, and in the final stages the person ceases to recognise the family or even the self in the mirror, loses bladder and bowel control, any capacity for self-care or ability to communicate in words. Thus social workers can help family and residential carers to understand this continuum, which for each person takes place against the background of previous memory, personality and life style. If family carers can describe to residential staff some of the way of life and habits of the dementia sufferer on admission, a routine can be worked out which closely resembles the previous pattern. For example, a well-ordered lady who had always prepared her husband's evening meal, was given the task of laying (and relaying) the tea tables to help with her restlessness at that time of day (Marshall, 1988).

For a social worker negotiating admission to a residential home for a dementia sufferer, it is particularly important to work out a contract, using a relative or friend if necessary to sign the contract and become the advocate on behalf of the client. This should include a care plan, following a pre-admission assessment. It would recognise the kind of behaviour pattern being presented, and build on the carer's experience of the best way of coping. Communicating the care plan and offering reassurance of how difficulties like incontinence would be dealt with, can ease the build-up of anxiety which dementia sufferers experience, about not being 'up to the mark'. Those with fluctuating dementia do have times of insight.

If a home were recognisably offering multiple regimes, this would offer dementia sufferers the opportunity to have a programme of care which included preventive toileting, more personal assistance, observation and structure to the day. A walk outside might help night restlessness more than medication. Family members may well want and need to continue to be closely involved, working to maintain previous personality with photographs, souvenirs, and mementoes. If a conversation gets started which taps into a flow of ideas from the past, sometimes this can be used to relate to current needs. It is as though one has to find and engage the kind of gear which will allow communication that day, recognising good days and bad. A recent upset or altercation can unsettle someone with severe dementia, making behaviour even more erratic. The feelings of dementia sufferers remain acute long after cognitive and behavioural impairment is clearly marked (Froggatt, 1988).

Ethnic minority elders   The triple jeopardy of those from ethnic minority groups, discussed in Chapter 3 extends to those elders whose families find they are unable to care for them. Residential living does need to feel comfortable; if the food and customs are inappropriate and the language incomprehensible then the elderly person is unlikely to settle down. There is at last discussion and pooling of ideas on how to make residential services accessible. For example, a day centre or residential home might have staff from the main minority groups. One of the cooks might be able to do kosher meals, another halal food, depending on the client group. A wing of a home might be set aside in this way, with potential residents and their families allowed to view the kitchen before admission to provide reassurance.

Residential staff need awareness of religious and cultural differences in terminal illness and death (Neuberger, 1987). In these various ways accommodation and services can be rearranged to offer suitability for different minority elders. The demand for places will not be there if the homes are not seen as suitable and families will struggle on (George and Young, 1986).

Death and dying   Some residents are likely to die while in residential care and there is a need for staff to have some training in helping to care for dying people, in supporting their families, and in attending to the feelings of other residents. It is noticeable when a resident withdraws from meals and sociability; the attention lavished on a dying resident is noted on the subtle residents' grapevine. Other residents are reassured or made more anxious by the degree of care surrounding the deaths in the home.

Again the needs of dying people of different faiths will increasingly have to be addressed and a social worker can offer knowledge and support to residential staff.

Private and voluntary residential homes

The increased provision of non-statutory residential care has already been noted. This extension of provision, encouraged by central government paying fees through supplementary benefit, drew a number of people of modest or no private means into the private sector. It is increasingly difficult for social workers to stand aloof. Local authority assessment of those funded by government spending has been recommended (Wagner, 1988).

Local authorities in England and Wales have a duty to register and inspect private homes under the 1984 Residential Homes Act, and apply a code of practice. In Scotland the Registered Establishments (Scotland) Act (1987) fulfills the same function. The regulations for private residential homes in Northern Ireland are contained in the Health and Personal Social Services (Northern Ireland) Order (1972), and the Health and Personal Social Services (Registration of Homes) Regulations (Northern Ireland) (1973). In 1988 the Department of Health and Social Security, Northern Ireland issued a 'Consultative paper on the Registration and Inspection of Private and Voluntary Residential and Nursing Homes' with a view to promoting a registered homes order in due course.

In all localities social workers introducing or visiting an elderly person in a private or voluntary Home have an overall responsibility for all residents, if there are disquieting indications to report (Marshall, 1988).

Private Homes are mostly small businesses, a cottage industry in the main (Weaver *et al.*, 1985). There is a sign that big businesses on either large scale or multiple units are moving into this market, thus leading to a need for even closer monitoring in view of the vulnerability of many residents. Some of the possible areas of exploitation were revealed in television programmes (Cook Report, 24.5.88; Granny Business YTV 1987).

Conditions for both residents and staff can be very good but can be poor. Where the proprietor and family undertake the night duty there may be proprietor 'burn out'. Unexpected overtime, low wages and complicated antisocial hours are features for many care assistants. This background is described so that social workers can encourage families to be aware of the pressures, and support their relatives by being closely involved. A resident without family, especially if mentally infirm, needs an advocate to negotiate with the home and to handle financial affairs through the Court of Protection (see Chapter 3).

Social work with residents and families

The area of work I am about to discuss is one in which relatively little social work time has been invested. Booth (1987) in a report investigating residential care in Camden emphasised how little priority is given by qualified field workers to developing their practice with old people around the issue of admission to residential homes. The examples of practice in this book especially Mrs R. (case study 5:1) show a social worker continuing to be involved once admission to care has taken place, and this kind of practice should be encouraged. The Wagner report (1988) suggests a nominated social worker should be involved with a client and family in all the decisions leading up to, and through any possible admission to care, whether it be day care, respite care, or eventual permanency after a trial period. Social work with residents and families might include monitoring and reviewing, counselling, negotiation, advocacy and group work.

Monitoring and reviewing

The system of a regular review for clients receiving day and respite care, demonstrated in case studies 2:2 and 5:2 show ways in which social workers can continue to provide links between the family network and the residential care establishment for those still living at home. The adoption of regular reviews for residents, requiring the continuing involvement of a social worker is gradually being implemented, but is slow to come in Homes for elderly people.

Counselling

As already suggested, the social worker should ensure that the principal carer, be this a relative or neighbour, visits the residential Home prior to the admission, accompanying the elderly person if this is wanted. The family need to feel that the reasons they can no longer support the relative in the community are recognised as valid. If residential staff can immediately encourage and welcome their continuing presence within the Home this eases some of the guilt. As described earlier, close involvement of a family member assists the major transition into a Home, and help with practical tasks such as unpacking, sorting out and explaining the daily routine helps to build a relationship between residential care staff, family, and the new resident. The role of the social worker in this aspect is as a facilitator, to make sure that this happens, for Homes differ in their practice.

Just as with childcare good practice requires social work help to provide a bridge between home and the new environment, so it is with vulnerable elderly people. Families too need a bridge, provided by social work help at this point. The mixed feelings at having given up the struggle to cope with the family member at home can lead to a diminution of visits, which may be painful at times. A social worker can support the family in hanging on through this pain, to recognise the major part still to be played. In the months and maybe years of life following admission to a residential Home there is time for much work of reparation, healing of old wounds and recollection of good experiences, provided there is continuity of contact. Of course the reverse may also be possible, that hostility and resentment build up, but this is all the more reason that a social worker should continue to be available for old people in residential care and the families.

Negotiation

In helping to negotiate a contract for a family member on admission there is scope for clarifying details of daily life, and helping the family and the old person work through their feelings about any restrictions. This contract should be reconsidered as the elderly person's progress or 'career' in the home is reviewed on a regular quarterly or half yearly basis, with the same social worker still responsible, and the family present or represented, along with the old person. This is the time for the social worker to help family members articulate their concerns, and how they would like to continue to be involved. For a very frail person, coming in to assist with eating tea once a week might be a family contribution. As frailty increases that kind of basic tending by the family may ease the terminal phase for everyone, practically and emotionally.

Advocacy

A social worker's relationship with a residential Home is through the introduction of a particular client and family. That should remain the primary focus, but as has been indicated there are other roles, connected with social service agency responsibility for standards in local authority, voluntary and private homes. These are roles of advocacy on the part of individual or collective needs, monitoring of standards in a general or specific way and of exercising occasional social control. It may be necessary to report back to management any concerns of mismanagement or potential abuse.

This is a delicate path to tread. Relatives are often fearful of complaining lest there is a backlash in the kind of treatment or care the family member receives. It is vital that the social worker does not get hooked into the same set of fears, nor slide into a collusion in supporting staff in their problems with management over staff shortages, overtime, and other organisational difficulties at the expense of meeting needs of residents.

Group work

Future development of social work practice in this area seems probable, with a social worker having responsibility for relating to a particular Home and its residents. This might offer more opportunity for group work with relatives or residents. In the setting of residential or day care, group work offers a social worker the chance to work with more people in a different way. It is possible to help a group share common concerns about experiencing another stage of oldness, or about being or becoming a resident. Some groups may be for information giving. The usual stages of group work, leading, planning, implementing, evaluating and following up a group should be followed (Preston-Shoot, 1987). It is essential to identify and work with any potential co-leader from the beginning. In addition in any institution other members of staff need to be kept fully informed about the purpose of the proposed group, and the practical details of place, time and membership. This helps to prevent disruption and facilitate attendance of the group members. While the proceedings of the group need to be kept confidential, other members of staff may need to be informed if there is distress in the group (Cooper, 1980).

Residents who want to participate in a group and share their experiences may find it easier if residential staff are not present, so that frankness can be risked. A relatives group may wish to share feelings about having an elderly family member admitted to a home, and explore their ongoing levels of involvement.

Conclusion

The kind of social work support to residents families and staff proposed in this chapter may already be practised by some social workers. Where such practice is not yet possible, encouragement is given by the Wagner report (1988) with the suggested role of a nominated social worker for each resident. It would improve the quality of life for residents, families and staff in residential care, to set clear goals. Through the provision of contracts on admission, and ongoing reviews of each resident's career in the Home, difficulties might be ironed out at an early stage.

If social workers do become integrated into Homes with a clear role offering continuity, the possibility of doing group work with residents and families should be considered. These different suggestions might help adjustment, self-esteem, and satisfaction for residents and their family members. It is hoped that residential care staff will continue to work closely with family members, to establish a different family network, replacing that which probably existed in the community.

7
Developing Community Networks

So far this book has focused on work with the vulnerable old person and his/her family in each situation. This chapter is about taking a wider view exploring ways of doing indirect social work to the benefit of later life families as a whole in a particular neighbourhood. That phrase 'indirect social work' is one adopted by the Barclay Report:

> It is clear that social workers spend some of their time in work which is not directly related to the problem of a particular ⟨client, but which is intended to assist groups of citizens to deal with their own problems, to create networks in localities or amongst those with similar social or medical problems, to sponsor self help, and to support individual and group attempts to offer help to those with social problems (Barclay, 1982, p. 20).

The Report goes on to describe indirect social work in a number of different ways, and as part of a wider view of social care planning. A full discussion of ways to do social care planning in the community is given by Payne (1986). Indirect social work can mean intervention with:

social support networks,
informal care networks;
volunteers;
self-help groups;
community social work/neighbourhood work;
community work;
developmental work and resource creation.

These kinds of indirect work, carried out by social workers at

108

different levels within social services, can be of value in work with vulnerable old people and their families, heightening social awareness and combating ageism, in many different sorts of community. The activities to be discussed here are those of maintaining social support networks, and informal care networks, sustaining volunteers, facilitating self help groups, and undertaking neighbourhood work.

Social support networks

These are the independent person's answer to some of the difficulties of old age. The essence of such a network is reciprocity, to be part of a set of interactions of close friends and family, where a set of trading relationships has been established. The work done by the research and development workers at the National Institute of Social Work, exploring networks for old people living alone, has shed light on the kinds of relationships which make a social support network effective (Crosbie *et al.*, 1982, p. 85; Sinclair *et al.*, 1984).

If social work in the community is to work at all, social workers need to develop skills in engaging, supporting, and aiding social support networks, as the first line of defence for vulnerable elderly people; this becomes the point at which the worker representing the formal care system interacts with the informal (unpaid) care system. Whittaker and Garbarino (1983, p. 5) say that 'A social support network is a set of interconnected relationships among a group of people that provides enduring patterns of nurturance – and provides contingent reinforcement for efforts to cope with life on a day to day basis'.

In other words an effective social support network has some elasticity in it. If an old person falls and is shaky for two or three days, the network will supply extra support, more meals and visits, until the brief crisis is over.

A social support network is marked by these three factors:

reciprocity;
sufficient energy;
openness of communication.

Reciprocity

The members of the network normally offer help to each other, even if the help takes different forms. For example two sisters lived in the same street on opposite sides of the road. Each had a key to the other's house. They spent much time popping back and forth. Unfortunately both showed signs of early mental impairment. The hazards of crossing the road, and the losing of keys brought this support network gradually to an end.

Sufficient energy

This is crucial for participation in a social support network. As with informal care, some people become seen as a local resource, and the weight of demands made upon them becomes too great. Then ambivalence builds up, about being involved in such a network.

Openness of communication

This third essential factor, means that members of a social support network must be able to exchange information about each other, or about the person a group are primarily supporting. Thus a reclusive very private old person is unlikely to have the benefit of such a network. These networks are mostly set up by people with no thought of social work involvement, as part of normal social interaction. It is possible to see how a social worker could facilitate establishing such a network, by introducing two neighbours in sheltered housing, newly moved in, or encouraging a reciprocal exchange of services between an old person and a single parent living very close, the old person undertaking babysitting, in return for having shopping done. Bingley and Waugh (1983) explored a social work role as key worker for nine old people living alone, only two of whom had local relatives. Ways were found for them to meet their needs for reciprocal involvement to stay in their own homes. Their care needs were met by statutory services, home helps and home care aides, but something more was needed, a social support network. Such a network can be appropriate to the culture and background of minority elderly people, so that extra informal support is also acceptable.

Social support networks have a wide variety of functions which help with the quality of life, for people of all ages. A worker can help a person identify the extent of the network, looking more broadly than just in terms of practical helping. The main functions of a network include providing a basis for the person to feel attached to others, to be involved with the community and helped to fit in, to have support for personal ideas and development, having others to turn to for guidance, advice and information, offering stability in relationships, to feel valued, a reassurance about self worth (Murgatroyd, 1985, p. 151). Additional roles for a professional helper have been identified within a network such as liaison, or acting as a mediator and information giver to change the gear of the relationship; for example it was possible to gain permission to tell the son and daughter-in-law of a very proud and independent old lady just how ill she was with cancer, so that they could share more fully in her feelings, and her planning of her life from then on (ibid.).

Informal care networks

There is obviously not a clear cut distinction between social support networks and informal care networks, except that the former presupposes a higher degree of personal independence for the old person concerned. Informal care networks have been studied, explored, expanded, funded and often interwoven into the formal statutory system of care (Bayley *et al.*, 1984; Sinclair *et al.*, 1984; Davies and Challis, 1986).

The mechanics of such interweaving need careful thought. First, the whole matter of intergenerational caring, of old care, or parent care, as described in Chapter 1, is still largely invisible, with many middle-aged carers feeling it is something they just have to get on with, a 'given' for them to do. There is an educative task to be done in focussing on the job informal carers do, to give them a higher profile. The ambivalence of carers may also need to be aired, and acknowledged. There is ignorance about what our cultural expectations are for caring. The present generation of carers, people in late fifties and sixties may be the last who feel that caring is something one has to do (Finch, 1987a). It might seem a positive step for a social worker to recruit extra informal carers in a complex situation. Care should be taken that in trying to solve a problem for which statutory resources are not available one is not taking

advantage of the willing or less than willing carer in the neighbourhood or family.

The main issues of working with informal networks of care have
been explored in the Networks Project (Sinclair *et al.*, 1984). First,
it seemed that social workers were preoccupied with quickly
achieving practical solutions to problems, finding it hard to focus on
the client's view of her/his situation, and taking time to work with
the client at a sensitive pace through the various possibilities. This is
time-consuming, and so is working with the informal networks of
care for it involves:

1   Contact with other professionals – multidisciplinary working.
2   Contacting carers and additional carers.
3   Problems of confidentiality. The importance of keeping in-
    formation confidential and of not colluding with other workers
    behind the client's back has been stressed already. However a
    different approach to confidentiality is needed in working with
    an informal care network. Having first secured the client's
    agreement to share information with the helpers it is necessary
    to keep on doing so, to keep in telephone communication with a
    list of helpers, for example to check the strain, pass on new
    information.
4   Sustaining networks by getting agreement as to who does what.
    This again takes time, for carers invest much of themselves in
    the care task, and can find it almost a snub or a criticism to have
    it suggested they do less, or do something differently, or take
    time out.
5   Handling conflict, an area identified as one social workers find
    difficult to deal with (Sinclair *et al.*, 1984, p. 41). Evasion,
    ignoring one of the parties involved, doing more of the work
    oneself, were all mechanisms for avoiding conflict. It should be
    recognised that strong well-established relationships and feelings
    about them are of the stuff of social work with clients in later life,
    and yet to move into a situation of conflict takes considerable
    courage, confidence, and not a little skill. The aura of age, the
    transference of feelings about one's own parents and grand-
    parents should they be in a similar situation adds to the difficulty
    for some workers. There is also the fear that relatives may be
    even more demanding of social work time than the client
    (Goldberg and Connelly, 1982, p. 98).

6 Sharing authority, another area to be considered in working with informal care networks. The social worker cannot do all the work personally. That indeed is the whole point of sustaining informal care networks. So informal carers have to be encouraged to rely on their own judgement, to have a certain authority (Bayley, 1982, p. 38). They may have to call up the home help organiser or social worker if the situation deteriorates or requires extra help from statutory resources.

7 Maintaining credibility means the social worker has to face several directions at once. He/she needs skill to present a case for additional resources when really required, so that her/his voice is heard without exaggerating in a way that undermines future credibility. There is a need to maintain that same credibility with the old person and the informal care network, not promising what cannot be delivered, whether it is services or regular support visits, yet responding promptly to a plea for help, or admission of strain. If it is possible to find funding for carers, as identified by the Kent Community Care Project, this might help to sustain a network. More than any thing carers need recognition for the job they do and to be backed up by relief from care and regular time for themselves. One way to assist is to facilitate a self help group for carers as discussed later in the chapter. These groups are often started and sustained by statutory workers, as well as voluntary agencies.

Volunteers

Working with volunteers is a vital part of sustaining informal care networks. Volunteers can often be found to help maintain a support system by freeing a carer for a few hours, or to undertake regular tasks such as driving someone to hospital for an appointment, driving client and carer to a carers support group meeting.

The widely known literature on volunteers (Holmes and Maizel, 1978; Payne, 1986; Ridley and Currie, 1987) has explored the problems of motivating and sustaining those who want to assist with informal caring. Social workers can get considerable help from volunteers for clients, but recruiting, training and supervising them takes time which needs to be acknowledged before embarking on such a programme. A support group/supervision session for a small group of volunteers so that they can report back is useful. Visiting a depressed lonely housebound person on a regular basis, far from being a simple task for an untrained person is in fact one of the most emotionally draining of activities; humans need interaction and reciprocity to feel good about themselves. Someone who has few visitors will fasten on the one person who appears and try to meet so many needs in that one visit. A volunteer is giving up time and effort and needs to know there is a valued purpose behind what is being done.

Time limited activities are useful, for example to ask a volunteer to take in a meal once a week for a month for an old person discharged from hospital and then to review this, before a new contract is worked out, or the volunteer moves to a new situation. Altruism is not enough for the volunteer; a purpose must be evident. It is this degree of organisation and support which makes it hard for social workers to get involved in the kind of quality of life improvements which volunteers can offer.

Self-help groups

These are started by a group of people who feel a common need, which they feel can be eased by sharing resources or information and personal support. Many self-help groups are around health issues, or disabilities. Social workers may wish to facilitate the start of a self-help group but before doing so some thought is needed (Payne, 1986; Ridley and Currie, 1987; Wilson, 1987). The main points to keep in mind are:

1   The amount of time the social worker has available as facilitator, and for how long?
2   What role is it appropriate for the social worker to have? It may help to start the group with a series of information giving meetings, but how will it proceed after that?
3   Structuring the group's aims and objectives may require some advice from the worker.
4   The content of discussion may at times become emotional or critical of available services. Can the worker cope with this? Should the worker attend all meetings?
5   The future programme, speakers, information, and contact with

other professional colleagues may also need some assistance from the worker.

6 Recognise the impermanent nature of self-help groups, reflecting other pressures on the participants. Those who organise self-help schemes have to be motivated by some unmet need of their own. Those most in need of relief may be too weary to organise (Wilson, 1987).

Self-help groups have played a crucial part in the maintenance of black communities, as available services are less likely to be appropriate. Ellice-Williams (1988) described: 'The helping tradition which cuts across the whole system of black culture.'

Religious institutions provide a particularly strong basis for such helping. The somewhat inappropriate services initially offered to black communities strengthened the need for self-help groups to care for old and mentally ill people within these communities.

Neighbourhood involvement

The Barclay report (1982, p. 43) had various names for the kind of social care planning it would like to see in the community: community development, indirect social work, neighbourhood work. Some social service departments operate a patch system (Hadley and McGrath, 1980) while others may have a community development sub-group. These kinds of activities should be distinguished from community work, which it is not possible to consider here. Research into neighbourhood work in Dinnington set out some parameters for establishing this kind of activity, wanting to set up informal networks of care. They found that a local base was needed with a population of about 10000, that co-operation was vital between statutory workers, in particular between home helps, wardens and social workers. Field social workers had to radically change their views of their work, and needed to be given much more autonomy.

> We still have to work very hard on the idea that it is valid for the workers to spend a lot of their time looking for, ferreting out and supporting the informal help which is already happening in the community (Bayley, 1982, p. 37; Seyd *et al.*,1984, p. 93).

The Dinnington Project demonstrated the kind of neighbourhood work being pioneered with an analysis of activities into five models of intervention:

person centred;
family centred;
network centred;
group centred;
neighbourhood centred.

Along with this they analysed six role clusters for social workers, which could form a matrix.

treatment agent;
teacher/counsellor;
broker;
advocate;
network system consultant;
entrepreneur/creator of resources.

In assisting a client in any situation the focus of attention may be on any one or more of the five modes of intervention, combined with any one or more of the roles. The flexibility of thought and action activated by this framework enabled the worker to replace an overloaded informal carer with formal and/or voluntary help; to move among parts of the neighbourhood system freely, knowing that it was all legitimated accountable work, supported by the agency (Bayley *et al.*, 1984).

This kind of network building involves knowing the key people in the community who know what is going on, who is ill or has not been seen. People doing milk or postal deliveries, in a sub-post office, or a corner shop might well value some training in what to look for, and whom to contact. It involves co-operating with the natural networks provided by churches, activity groups and old peoples' clubs. These are the kind of neighbours people turn to in times of trouble quite as much as physical neighbours, where there is much more reserve built into the relationship because of proximity (Abrams, 1978, p. 85).

Neighbourhood social work gives autonomy to home helps and street wardens to respond on an ad hoc basis to the needs of old people among whom they may live as well as work. A semi-formalised delegation of authority was pioneered in Nottingham

(Beaver, 1987). Again problems of confidentiality have to be discussed and clarified. It must be emphasised that this sharing of responsibility and authority, the delegation downwards, is of the essence of neighbourhood involvement for social workers.

For vulnerable elderly people and their families, a neighbourhood development project offers further support at grass roots level, helping to lessen the possible isolation of carer and cared for, tied into a household alone.

Conclusion

In this chapter emphasis has been put on indirect social work, rather than direct work with elderly people and their families. If social support networks, informal care networks, volunteers and self-help groups are to be enhanced and sustained as a part of the pattern of community care for vulnerable old people, social workers need to have these responsibilities acknowledged by their line managers. In areas where neighbourhood social work is being practised that may be relatively easy. Moving from a case based form of activity to community social work as an individual worker may be more difficult. Some of the suggestions outlined here may give encouragement to take some risks to develop wider skills in consultation with others.

8

Professional, Public and Personal

In drawing together the threads that have interwoven the discussion in this book three sets of issues stand out distinctly, namely the professional, the public and the personal aspects of work with vulnerable elderly people and their families. For clarity these are separated but inevitably and properly the interweaving of these issues offers the specialism of social work with old people its strength.

Professional issues

As a result of the increase in the proportion of very old people to those of working age, there is an increase in demand for social care for some elderly people in the latter stages of disability and dependency. This presents an enlarged arena of welfare practice, working with carers and cared for in their own homes. While social work has much to offer in these situations a much wider group of professionals, semi-professional and untrained workers are likely to continue to be involved in the care of old people at risk, than are concerned with children at risk. The place of social work within this consortium of care needs careful identification and maintenance. Social workers could be effective in helping to provide good quality social care for cared for and carers if there was some alteration in organisational priorities.

Professions within welfare are simultaneously changing and shifting and changing boundaries. Social work has been so preoccupied with the issues and demands of child protection that it has almost overlooked the possibility of becoming closely incorporated with

118

primary health care, particularly for groups of clients, who are disabled, handicapped or very old. Pioneering research suggests this is the way forward (Goldberg, 1987). The nursing profession has expanded its understanding of patients as people; community psychiatric nurses, mental handicap nurses and health visitors, together with para-medical professionals, physiotherapists and occupational therapists prove ready and willing to enter the arena of social care, and especially that for vulnerable elderly people, offering specialist expertise and skilled counselling.

There is all the more reason to reclarify the main aspects of social work practice with elderly clients and their families, namely client participation, family support, sustaining the network, the case manager role, implications for managers, and issues for education and training.

Client participation

Emphasis here has been put on ways of working which focus on a vulnerable elderly person as a continuing participant, rather than a passive recipient, in obtaining social care. The social support network, incorporating relationships built up over time, forms the core of the care received by most old people, who must normally make a response in some way, either practically, financially or emotionally if the network is to be maintained.

Those who seek help from social services departments mostly come from particularly complex situations which have outworn the local support system. The Networks Project in London discovered that:

> Most of the social work clients fell into two groups very roughly the 'difficult' and the 'disabled'. The difficult were hard to help because of their personalities; the disabled because of the extent of their practical needs (Sinclair *et al.*, 1984).

Thus clients of social service departments, and particularly those who are deemed to need social work support as well as services are more likely to be housebound, or socially isolated without family nearby, mentally infirm and confused, or severely disabled, with low morale and loneliness a major factor in many situations.

Energising such a person to feel some sense of hope and purpose once again, does require skill, and is psychologically demanding work. The principal objective should remain clear, to respect individuality and enable a vulnerable elderly client to make positive choices about the future, taking into account the views of members of the family network.

Support for families

Families at this stage may well be feeling guilty and uncertain how to proceed with their responsibilities. It has been suggested (Eyde and Rich, 1983) that social work goals should include:

1   ways to decrease dependency of the elderly person;
2   ways to increase the predictability and stability of what the family can offer;
3   ways to decrease anxiety and stress around care giving, building skills and confidence;
4   ways of increasing knowledge about normal and atypical care-giving situations, and the services needed and available;
5   ways of respecting personal and family boundaries;
6   ways of helping the family to pace the level of care and stimulation they offer to the elderly person so that what is offered is not overwhelming and over stimulating.

Sustaining the network

It has become increasingly clear that helping old people to continue in their own environment for as long as possible can best be done by a social work approach which is actively working to secure and maintain social support networks. This aspect of preventive social work is one which it may be hard to achieve where social service organisation is based on an area office rather than a 'patch' organisation.

Yet in every situation, once a vulnerable old person has been referred, identification of the network should be a major task within assessment, and maintaining that network part of the monitoring aspect of social care planning. Indirect social work features prominently in work with old people and their families.

Case managers

The role for social workers as case managers identified by the Kent Community Care Project (Davies and Challis, 1986), and reinforced by Griffiths (1988) has already been discussed. This role appears under slightly different titles and frameworks in other projects as 'care manager', 'care co-ordinator', 'key worker'. It does require the devolution of some managerial responsibility, accountability and financial control. This is to allow the social worker to buy in the resources needed to provide the care required at home, whether this be home help, day care, day or night sitting services, respite care, or regular payments to neighbours to perform selected tasks on a regular basis.

Devolution of responsibility to family and formal carers such as home helps may also be required, necessitating in-service training for employees.

The case manager role is one which need not be undertaken by a social worker as the Darlington Project showed (Stone, 1987). Yet the psychological understanding which social workers bring has been regarded as a particularly valuable contribution – 'The Heineken effect' (Davies and Knapp, 1988).

As a case manager indirect social work is required to sustain volunteers, carers and home care aides. The complex relationships in later life families will continue to form a feature of social work with vulnerable elderly people; this may mean enabling and training other workers to recognise and cope with painful, ambivalent, hostile or guilty feelings.

Organisational implications

There are three main ways forward to enhance social work with elderly people and their families. These involve some organisational changes involving the support and agreement of all levels of management.

One involves the 'structured specialism' defined by Goldberg (1987) building on the case manager role, including devolved financial accountability for social workers. Another profession may step in to take on these responsibilities if social workers are not prepared or not allowed to do so.

Another alternative, where community social work has been established or is planned, offers social workers a chance to exercise devolved managerial responsibility in a different way, using indirect social work. In place of direct face to face work with all clients, the social worker would work with carers, volunteers, and other professionals, maintaining social support networks. The most immediately obvious way to facilitate social work with elderly people is for team leaders to allocate individual cases to social workers and supervise some complex cases as a high priority, along the lines suggested here.

Training in social care

As indicated, social workers may find themselves in the role of 'trainers' of colleagues. The distinction between trained and untrained, qualified and unqualified workers will continue to be blurred in providing social care. Those formally engaged in training for social care already recognise this. Some open courses in community care already attract a wide range of formal and informal carers. Care assistants, home helps, and family carers may all be found in evening classes finding out more about resources and techniques for coping. The National Council for Vocational Qualifications validates courses in social care. Dissemination of the understanding of the complexities of later family life will be needed at many levels.

Education and training in social work with elderly people

It is probably pretentious to use the term 'gerontological social work' to describe work with later life families and their vulnerable members. However, the degree of skill required of social workers justifies the creation and recognition of a specialism, which is aided by a distinctive title.

In seeking to specialise in work with elderly people social workers have to move forward on five main fronts:

1   Developing understanding and knowledge of the impact of dependency needs in later life families, across a range of cultures in a multiracial society.

2   Being able to share understanding and responsibility appropriately when practising indirect social work with formal and
family carers who make up social support networks.
3   Learning to develop a wide range of personal skills as a social
worker which draw on a full range of methods of intervention.
This requires taking some risks and being ready to experiment,
in transferring skills learned with younger families and groups to
later life members.
4   Pressing for training for senior and middle management in
changing patterns of social work practice and service delivery
for elderly clients. This will be as necessary as training for face to
face practitioners. Organisations have their own inbuilt inertia;
without recognition of the need for a different structure little
change will be possible.
5   To combat ageism, being prepared to offer a high profile to
social work with elderly people, developing pioneering and
defending policy and worthwhile initiatives.

Public issues

The issues to be addressed include ageism, organisational change,
and the future provision of family care for elderly people. The
public attitude to very old people, the prevalent ageism which is not
even recognised as such, gives social work here a very uphill
struggle. For example, a cartoon put out by a local authority to
advocate its bulk removal service depicted a refuse collector strug-
gling along carrying a moth eaten armchair on his back, on which sat
a knitting granny. The caption read: 'To get rid of your bulky
rubbish call the junk line. It will be taken away.' The poster was
withdrawn after protests about sexism. The ageism was not even
recognised. This also illustrates the double jeopardy of elderly
women, twice stigmatised.

It appears that the principles of social work may have been
reformulated in the case of old age: 'The principle that social work
should be unconditional, that is not related to the likely return . . .
has become transformed by a concept of useful investment of effort
to the detriment of elderly people' (Norman, 1987b). The attention
that is paid to work with old people tends to focus on managerial
efficiency, organisation and financial accountability (Audit
Commission, 1985; Griffiths, 1988).

Building on the quest for managerial efficiency, ways have been suggested to devolve responsibility downwards so that decision-making about service delivery takes place much closer to clients and their family networks. Whether family care will continue to be available for the increased number of dependent elderly people remains somewhat uncertain. There is a strong moral imperative, particularly among women, to take responsibility for their kin. But the preferred pattern among women and among old people is for some sort of 'intimacy at a distance'. Professional services will be sought to give relief. Finch (1987b) who has considered these matters carefully concluded: 'Women must have the right not to care, and dependent people must have the right not to rely on their relatives.'

The recognition that there are likely to be six million carers in the country (Green, 1988) should give carers more clout in demanding and getting the necessary back-up in assessment, technological aids, services and counselling to enable them to carry through their caring responsibilities without undue strain. Before the caring becomes an intolerable burden it should be possible to relinquish or share the day to day labour of caring without feeling guilty, knowing good quality care is available.

The low status and low pay of formal carers in rest homes, hospitals and in the community is a further aspect that needs to be borne in mind, particularly in crises over residential care. In both residential and field work with elderly people, the least powerful and least qualified staff are given major responsibilities to do the work (Quigley and Womphrey, 1988).

Personal issues

One of the threads identified throughout the book has been how private feelings of ambivalence, mixed affection and dread of intimacy with extreme old age affect the work of professionals, encouraging a withdrawal from this area of work. Coming to terms with death, grief and loss in a personal sense, as a result of coping with family pressures at home puts many professionals in a double or triple bind when working with elderly people and their families. The complexities and emotional demands may seem inescapable and overwhelming. Personal counselling outside the work setting to explore some of these issues offers professionals a way to cope, as in other areas of painful bombardment. In offering to take on other people's pain strength comes from acknowledging one's personal vulnerability and humanity.

Social work with later life families and vulnerable elders may be technically less complicated than child care work in that there is a less elaborate statutory framework. Emotionally it can be extremely demanding, in that many referrals arise because the family network has run out of solutions and the situation is almost intolerable. The impact of the work may trigger off unexpected reactions in the worker; the need for supervision and consultation within the work setting remains essential to the development of good practice. This brings us back again to the high professional standards needed.

Conclusion

Many of the problems with which social workers struggle are simultaneously structural, sociological and psychological, reflecting changes in relationships within families, society and the economy of the country. It may be difficult to work with elderly people but it should not be boring. It is daunting work for it requires anticipation and preparation for one's own ageing processes and that of one's family, in order to empathise with aged disabled clients. It requires imaginative empathy, too, to overcome communication difficulties with clients, and with colleagues from other professions.

It requires respect for the moral and legal rights of cared for people and their carers, and thus a readiness to enter into situations of conflict. It requires a capacity to stand up to the requirements of social service departments for efficiency and cost effectiveness. Both competing for scarce resources, and pressing for additional services are involved. Sometimes it may be necessary to allow a situation to break down to prevent intolerable stress being put on family carers.

A broad spectrum of skills are needed across the breadth of social work expertise, in individual, family, group, and neighbourhood work. These should be used in such a way that elderly clients and their families retain some sense of still being in control of their own lives, when seeking social service assistance.

We have to remember too that this area of work is not one that can be too tidy. Tolerance of muddle and of human frailties can be accompanied by warmth and affection in helping people retain a zest for living. Provided vulnerable old people are left with some choices, some areas where they can exercise individuality and remember themselves as people of consequence and value, then we are showing respect. There is scope then for creativity in action, for sensitivity in change, recognising the subtleties of experience that people go through in times of anxiety and stress in the ageing and dying process.

References

Abrams, P. (1978) 'Community Care: Some Research Problems and Priorities', in Barnes, J. and Connelly, N. *Social Care Research*, London, Bedford Square Press for Policy Studies Institute.

Abrams, S. and Marsden, D. (1987) in Allat, A., Kell, T., Bryman, A. and Bytheway, B. (eds), *Women and the Life Cycle: Transitions and Turning Points*, London, Macmillan.

Age Concern (1986) *The Law and Vulnerable Elderly People*, London, Age Concern.

Allen, I. (1983) 'The Elderly and Their Informal Carers', in Department of Health and Social Security, *Elderly People in the Community: Their Service Needs*, London, HMSO.

Audit Commission (1985) *Managing Social Services for the Elderly More Effectively*, London, HMSO.

Audit Commission (1986) *Making a Reality of Community Care*, London, HMSO.

Avebury, K. (Chairperson) (1984) *Home Life: A Code of Practice for Residential Care*, London, Centre for Policy on Ageing.

Bakur-Weiner, M. and Taggart White, M. (1982) 'Depression as the Search for a Lost Self', *Psychotherapy Theory Research and Practice*, 19, 4, 491–9.

Barclay, P. (ed.) (1982) *Social Workers, their Role and Tasks*, London, National Institute of Social Work with Bedford Square Press.

Bayley, M. (1982) 'Community Care and the Elderly', in Glendinning, F. (ed.) op. cit.

Bayley, M., Parker, P., Seyd, R. and Tennant, A. (1984) *Dinnington Project Final Report*, Sheffield, University of Sheffield Joint Unit for Social Services Research.

Bayley, M., Parker, P. Seyd R. and Tennant A. (1987) *Practising Community Care: Developing Locally Based Practice*, Sheffield, University of Sheffield Joint Unit for Social Services Research.

Beaver, R. (1987) 'Decentralisation of Domiciliary Services', paper presented at Conference on the Future of Adult Life, Leiden, Netherlands.

Bhalla, A. and Blakemore, K. (1981) *Elders of the Minority Ethnic Groups*, Birmingham, AFFOR.

127

Bingley, E. and Waugh, M. (1983) 'Staying at Home', *Community Care*, No. 451, 19–21.

Birrell, D. and Williamson, I. (1983) 'Northern Ireland's Integrated Health and Personal Social Services Structure', in Williamson, A. and Room, G. (eds) *Health and Welfare States of Britain*, London, Heinemann Educational.

Black, J., Bowl, R., Burns, D., Critcher, C. and Stockford, D. (1983) *Social Work in Context*, London, Tavistock.

Blenkner, M. (1965) 'Social Work and Family Relationships in Later Life with Some Thoughts on Filial Maturity', in Shanas, E. and Streub, G. (eds), *Social Structure and the Family*, New York, Prentice Hall.

Bogo, M. (1987) 'Social Work Practice with Family Systems in Admission to Homes for the Aged', *Journal of Gerontological Social Work*, 10, 1/2, 5–10.

Booth, T. (1987) 'Camden Shows the Way', *Community Care*, No. 649, 16–17.

Booth, T. (1985) *Home Truths*, London, Gower.

Booth, T., Barritt A., Berry, S., Martin D., Melotte C. and Phillips D. (1982) 'Dependency: Challenging the Myths', *Community Care*, 434, 17–19.

Boyd, W. (Chairperson) (1988) *Dementia and the Law: the Challenge Ahead*, Edinburgh, Scottish Action on Dementia.

Bradford Brown, B. and Chang, Chi-Pang (1983) 'Drug and Alcohol Abuse Among the Elderly', *International Journal of Aging and Human Development*, 18, 1, 1–12.

Brearley, C. P. (1982) *Risk and Ageing*, London, Routledge & Kegan Paul.

Buckle, J. (1981) *Intake Teams*, London, Tavistock.

Burton, A. and Dempsey, J. (1988) 'Dementia and Guardianship', *Social Work Today*, 20, 4, 14–15.

Butler, R. and Lewis, M. (1982) *Aging and Mental Health*, 3rd edn, St Louis, London, C.V. Mosby.

Caplan, G. (1961) *An Approach to Community Health*, London, Tavistock.

Carver, V. and Liddiard, P. (1978) *An Ageing Population*, London, Hodder and Stoughton with Open University.

Challis, D. (1982) 'Towards More Creative Social Work with the Elderly: the Community Care Project', in Glendinning, F. (ed.) op. cit.

Challis, D. and Davies, B. (1985) 'Long Term Care for the Elderly: the Community Care Scheme', *British Journal of Social Work*, 15, 6, 563–80.

Charlesworth, A., Wilkin, D. and Durie, A. (1984) *Carers and Services: a Comparison of Men and Women Caring for Dependent Elderly People*, Manchester Equal Opportunities Commission.

Cloke, C. (1983) *Old Age Abuse in the Domestic Setting*, London, Age Concern.

Clough, R. (1981) *Old Age Homes*, London, George Allen & Unwin.

Coleman, P. (1986) *Ageing and Reminiscence Processes*, London, John Wiley.

Cooper, J. (1980) *Social Group Work with Elderly People in Hospital*, Keele, Beth Johnson Foundation and University of Keele.

Corden, J. and Preston-Shoot, M. (1987) *Contracts in Social Work*, Aldershot, Gower.

Crosbie, D., O'Connor, P. and Vickery, A. (1982) 'Working with an Area Team: Research and Development in Networks for the Elderly', in Glendinning, F. (ed.) op. cit.

Crosbie, D. (1983) 'A Role for Anyone?', *British Journal of Social Work*, 13, 2, 123–49.

Coulshed, V. (1988) *Social Work Practice: An Introduction*, London, Macmillan.

Dalley, G. (1988) *Ideologies of Caring*, London, Macmillan Educational.

Davies, B. (1987) 'Equity and Efficiency in Community Care: Supply and Financing in an Age of Fiscal Austerity', *Ageing and Society*, 7, 2, 161–74.

Davies, B. and Challis, D. (1986) *Matching Resources to Needs in Community Care*, Aldershot, Gower.

Davies, B. and Knapp, M. (1988) 'Costs and Residential Social Care', in Sinclair, I. (ed.) op. cit.

Deeping, E. (1979) *Caring for Elderly Parents*, London, Constable.

Department of Health and Social Security (DHSS) (1981), *Growing Older*, Cmnd 8173, London, HMSO.

Dierking, B., Brown, M. and Fortune, A. (1980) 'Task Centred Treatment in a Residential Facility for the Elderly', *Journal of Gerontological Social Work*, 2, 3, 225–40.

Eastman, M. (1984) *Old Age Abuse*, Mitcham Age Concern, England.

Ellice-Williams, R. (1988) 'Community Care: the Invisible Vanguard', *Social Work Today*, 19, 40, 21.

England, H. (1986) *Social Work as Art*, London, Allen & Unwin.

Equal Opportunities Commission (EOC) (1980) *The Experience of Caring for Elderly and Handicapped Dependents: Survey Report*, Manchester Equal Opportunities Commission.

Equal Opportunities Commission (EOC) (1982) *Caring for the Elderly and Handicapped*, Manchester, Equal Opportunities Commission.

Erikson, E. (1965) *Childhood and Society*, Harmondsworth, Penguin.

Erikson, E. (1978) *Adulthood*, New York, W.W. Norton.

Evans, D. (1985) 'Twosomes and Threesomes: Family Therapy with the Elderly', *Community Care*, 547, 16–8.

Evers, H. (1981) 'Care or Custody: the Experiences of Women Patients in Long Stay Wards', in B. Hutter and G. Williams (eds), op. cit.

Evers, H. (1983) 'Elderly Women and Disadvantage: Perceptions of Daily Life and Support Relationships' in D. Jerrome (ed.), *Ageing in Modern Society*, London, Croom Helm.

Eyde, D. and Rich, J. (1983) *Psychological Distress in Aging*, Rockville, Md, Aspen Systems.

Finch, J. (1987a) 'Family Ties', *New Society*, 82, 1264.

Finch, J. (1987b) 'Whose Responsibility? Women and the Future of Family Care', in *Informal Care Tomorrow*, London, Policy Studies Institute.

Finch, J. (1987c) 'Family Obligations and the Life Course', in Bryman, A., Allat, A., Kell, T. and Bytheway, B. (eds), *Rethinking the Life Cycle*, London, Macmillan.

Finch, J. and Groves, D. (1983) *A Labour of Love*, London, Routledge & Kegan Paul.

Fogarty, M. (1975) *Forty to Sixty*, London, Bedford Square Press for the Centre for Studies in Social Policy.

Ford, J. (1988) 'Negotiation (Counselling and Advocacy): A Response to Bill Jordan, *British Journal of Social Work*, 18, 1, 57–62.

Fortune, A. and Rathbone McCuan, E. (1981) 'Education in Gerontological Social Work: Application of the Task Centred Model', *Journal of Education for Social Work*, 17, 3, 98–105.

Froggatt, A. (1975) 'Listening to the Voices of Older Women', in Butler, A. (ed.), *Ageing: Recent Advances and Creative Responses*, London, Croom Helm.

Froggatt, A. (1988) 'Self-Awareness in Early Dementia', in Gearing, B., Johnson, M. and Heller, T. (eds), op. cit.

Garbarino, J. (1986) 'Where Does Social Support Fit?' *British Journal of Social Work*, 16, Supplement.

Gearing, B., Johnson, M. and Heller, T. (eds) (1988) *Mental Health Problems in Old Age*, Chichester, John Wiley.

Geroge, J. and Young, J. (1986) 'Elderly Asians with Stroke: a Particular Challenge', *Geriatric Medicine*, 16, 19–21.

Glendinning, F. (ed.) (1982) *Care in the Community: Recent Research and Current Projects*, Keele, Beth Johnson Foundation and University of Keele.

Glendinning, F. (1987) *Social Work with Elderly People: New Perspectives*, Keele, Beth Johnson Foundation and University of Keele.

Godlove, C., Richard, L. and Rodwell, G. (1982) *Time for Action*, Sheffield, University of Sheffield Joint Unit for Social Services Research.

Goldberg, E. M. and Connelly, N. (1982) *The Effectiveness of Social Care for the Elderly*, London, Policy Studies Institute with Heinemann Educational.

Goldberg, E. M. (1987) 'The Effectiveness of Social Care: A Selective Exploration', *British Journal of Social Work*, 17, 6, 595–614.

Goldstein, H. (1977) *Social Work Practice: A Unitary Approach*, Columbia, University of South Carolina Press.

Goodman, C. and Ward, M. (1988) 'Age and Alcohol: a Dangerous Cocktail', *Community Care*, no. 736, 16–17.

Goodstein, R. K. (1982) 'Individual Psychotherapy and the Elderly', *Psychotherapy Theory Research and Practice*, 19, 4, 412–8.

Gorell Barnes, G. (1984) *Working with Families*, London, Macmillan.

Gould, R. L. (1978) *Transformations: Growth and Change in Adult Life*, New York, Simon & Schuster.

Graham, H. (1983) 'A Labour of Love', in Finch, J. and Groves, D. (eds), op. cit.

Graham, H. (1984) *Women, Health and Family*, Brighton, Wheatsheaf Books Harvester Press.

Grant, L. (1988) 'Black Elderly: the Caribbean Perspective', in Mossadeq, M. and Froggatt, A. (eds) op. cit.

Gray, B. and Isaacs, B. (1979) *Care of the Elderly Mentally Infirm*, London, Tavistock.

Green, H. (1988) *Informal Carers: General Household Survey 1985*, London, HMSO.

Greene, R. (1986) *Social Work with the Aged and their Families*, New York, Aldine de Gruyter.

Griffiths, R. (1988) *Community Care: Agenda for Action*, London, HMSO.

Hadley, R. and McGrath, M. (1984) *When Social Services are Local*, London, George Allen & Unwin.

Harper, S. (1987) 'The Kinship network of Rural Aged', *Ageing and Society*, 3, 303–28.

Health Advisory Service (1983) *The Rising Tide*, London, Department of Health and Social Security.

Hemmings, S. (1985), *A Wealth of Experience*, London, Pandora Press.

Hickey, T. (1981) 'Neglect and Abuse of Older Family Members', *Gerontologist*, 21, 2, 171–6.

Holman, R. (1986) 'The Plight of a Pensioner', *Community Care*, no. 640, 20–1.

Holmes, A. and Maizel, J. (1978) *Social Work and Volunteers*, London, George Allen & Unwin with BASW.

Howe, D. (1986) *Social Workers and their Practice in Welfare Bureaucracies*, Aldershot, Gower.

Hunt, A. (1978) *The Elderly at Home*, London, HMSO.

Hunter, J. (1983) 'The Last Use of Time', *New Age*, 21, 17.

Huntingdon, J. (1981) *Social Work and General Medical Practice*, London, Allen & Unwin.

Hutter, B. and Williams, G. (1981) *Controlling Women: The Normal and the Deviant*, London, Croom Helm.

Isaacs, B. (1980) 'Burden of Care', *New Age*, 12, 23–25.

Isaacs, B. and Neville, Y. (1976) 'The Needs of Old People: The Interval as a Method of Measurement', *British Journal of Preventive and Social Medicine*, 30, 2, 79–85.

Itzin, C. (1984) 'Learning Oppression. Links Between Ageism, Sexism and Adultism, unpublished paper presented at British Society of Gerontology Conference, University of Leeds.

Jerrome, D. (1982) 'Men, Women and Friendship in Old Age', unpublished paper presented at British Society of Gerontology Conference, University of Hull.

Jordan, B. (1987) 'Counselling Advocacy and Negotiation', *British Journal of Social Work*, 2, 17, 135–46.

Kelly, D. (1987) 'Letters from those Who Receive Care', *Social Work Today*, 18, 22, 24.

Kinney, M., Wendt, R. and Hurst, J. (1988) 'Elder abuse: issues, treatment and support', in B. Gearing *et al.* op. cit.

Levin, E., Sinclair, I. and Gorbach, P. (1984) *The Supporters of Confused at Home*, London, National Institute of Social Work.

Lieberman, S. (1979) *Transgenerational Family Therapy*, London, Croom Helm.
Macdonald, B. with Rich, C. (1984) *Look Me in the Eye*, London, Women's Press.
Marshall, M. (1983) *Social Work with Old People*, London, Macmillan.
Marshall, M. (ed.) (1988) *Guidelines for Social Workers Working with People with Dementia and Their Carers*, Birmingham, British Association of Social Workers.
Maslow, A. H. (1970) *Motivation and Personality*, 2nd edn, New York, Harper & Row.
Mattinson, J. and Sinclair, I. (1979) *Mate and Stalemate*, Oxford, Blackwell and Tavistock.
Minuchin, S. with Fishman, H. C. (1981) *Family Therapy Techniques*, London and Cambridge, Mass., Harvard University Press.
Mossadeq, M. and Froggatt, A. (1988) *Black and Asian Elders: Do Our Services Deliver?* Report of Conference, University of Bradford and Bradford Social Services Directorate.
Murgatroyd, S. (1985) *Counselling and Helping*, London and New York, British Psychological Society and Methuen.
Murphy, E. (1983) 'Old Age and Depression in the East End of London', *New Age*, 21, 22–4.
Neuberger, J. (1987) *Caring for Dying People of Different Faiths*, London, Lisa Sainsbury Foundation and Austen Cornish Publishers.
Neugarten, B. (1968) *Middle Age and Aging*, Chicago, University of Chicago Press.
Newman, J. L. (1978) 'Old Folk in Wet Beds', in Carver V. and Liddiard P. (eds) op. cit.
Newton, E. (1980) *This Bed My Centre*, London, Virago.
Nissell, M. and Bonnerjea, L. (1982) *Family Care of the Handicapped Elderly: Measuring the Cost*, London Policy Studies Institute.
Norman, A. (1985) *Triple Jeopardy*, London, Centre for Policy on Ageing.
Norman, A. (1987a) *Severe Dementia: the Provision of Long Stay Care*, London, Centre for Policy on Ageing.
Norman, A. (1987b) *Aspects of Ageism*, London, Centre for Policy on Ageing.
Office of Population Censuses and Surveys (OPCS) (1984) *General Household Survey 1982*, London, HMSO.
Office of Population Censuses and Surveys (OPCS) (1986) *General Household Survey*, Preliminary Results for 1985, *OPCS Monitor*, September.
O'Hagan, K. (1986) *Crisis Intervention in Social, Services*, London, Macmillan.
Palazzoli, M. S., Boscolo, L. and Cecchin, G. (1980) 'Hypothesising-Circularity-Neutrality: Three Guidelines for the Conductor of the Session', *Family Process*, 19, 1, 3–12.
Parker, R. (1981) 'Tending and Social Policy', in E. M. Goldberg and S. Hatch (eds), *A New Look at the Personal Social Services*, London, Policy Studies Institute.
Parkes, C. M. (1986) *Bereavement: Studies of Grief in Adult Life*, 2nd edn,

Harmondsworth, Penguin.

Payne, M. (1986) *Social Care in the Community*, London, Macmillan.

Peace, S. (1986) 'The Forgotten Female: Social Policy and Older Women', in Phillipson, C. and Walker, A. (eds), op. cit.

Phillipson, C. (1981) 'Women in Later Life', in Hutter, B. and Williams, G. (eds), op. cit.

Phillipson, C. (1982) *Capitalism and the Construction of Old Age*. London, Macmillan.

Phillipson, C. and Walker A. (1986) *Ageing and Social Policy*, Aldershot, Gower.

Pincus, A. and Minahan, A. (1973) *Social Work Practice: Model and Method*, Itaxa, Ill., Peacock.

Pincus, L. (1981) *The Challenge of a Long Life*, London, Faber.

Pottle, S. (1984) 'Developing a Network-oriented Service for Elderly People and their Carers', in Treacher, A. and Carpenter, J. (eds), *Using Family Therapy*, Oxford, Blackwell.

Preston-Shoot, M. (1987) *Effective Group Work*, London, Macmillan.

Quigley, G. and Womphrey, J. (1988) 'Violence Can Never be Justified' *Community Care*, no. 716, 20–1.

Qureshi, H. and Walker, A. (1986) 'Caring for Elderly People: the Family and the State' in Phillipson, C. and Walker, A. (eds), op. cit.

Rack, P. (1982) *Race Culture and Mental Disorder*, London, Tavistock.

Rawlings, S. C. (1988) 'Raising Standards with Network Meetings', *Social Work Today*, 19, 28.

Reid, W. J. and Epstein, L. (1977) *Task Centred Practice*, New York, Columbia University Press.

Richards, M. (1987) 'Developing the Context of Practice Teaching', *Social Work Education*, 6, 2, 4–9.

Ridley, J. and Currie, R. (1987) *Towards a Better Partnership: Social Workers and Volunteers*, Birmingham, British Association of Social Workers.

Rimmer, L. (1981) *Families in Focus: Marriage, Divorce and Family Patterns*, London, Study Commission on the Family.

Roberts, A. (1988) 'Alcohol and Elderly People', *Nursing Times*, 84, 8, 49–52.

Rogers, C. (1967) *On Becoming a Person*, London, Constable.

Rossiter, C. and Wicks, M. (1982) *Crisis or Challenge: Family Care Elderly People and Social Policy*, London, Study Commission on the Family.

Seebohm, F. (Chairperson) (1968) *Report into Local Authority and Allied Social Services*, Cmnd 3703, London, HMSO.

Seyd, R., Tennant, A., Bayley, M. and Parker, P. (1984) *Community Social Work*, Sheffield, Neighbourhood Services Project, Dinnington Paper No. 8, Sociological Studies, University of Sheffield.

Sher, M. (1983) 'Psychodynamic Work with Clients in the Latter Half of Life', *Journal of Social Work Practice*, 1, 1, 56–71.

Sinclair, I. (ed.) (1988a) *Residential Care: the Research Reviewed*, London, National Institute for Social Work/HMSO.

Sinclair, I. (1988b) 'Residential Care for Elderly People', in Sinclair,

134   *Family Work with Elderly People*

I. (ed.) op. cit.
Sinclair, I., Crosbie, D., O'Connor, P., Stanforth, L. and Vickery, A. (1984) *Networks Project:* A study of informal services and social work for elderly clients living alone, London, National Institute of Social Work Research Unit.
Skinner, R. (1988) 'Young at Heart', *Community Care*, no. 698, 24–5.
Solomon, R. (1982) 'Serving Families of the Institutionalised Aged', *Journal of Gerontological Social Work*, 5, 1/2, 83–96.
Sontag, S. (1978) 'The Double Standard of Ageing', in Carver, V. and Liddiard, P. (eds), op. cit.
Specht, H. and Vickery, A. (eds), (1979) *Integrating Social Work Methods*, London, Allen & Unwin.
Squires, A. (ed.) (1988) *Rehabilitation of the Older Patient*, London, Croom Helm.
Stapleton, B. (1979) 'Avoiding Residential Care for the Old', *Community Care*, no. 263, 14–6.
Starr, B. D. and Bakur-Weiner, M. (1982) *The Starr–Weiner Report on Sex and Sexuality in the Mature Years*, New York, McGraw-Hill.
Stone, M. (1987) *Darlington Community Care Project: Integrating Health and Social Care at the Client Level for the Frail Elderly*, Canterbury University of Kent Personal Social Services Research Unit.
Strean, H. (1983) *The Sexual Dimension*, New York, Free Press Macmillan.
Tobin, S. and Lieberman, M. (1976) *Last Home for the Aged*, San Francisco and London, Jossey-Bass.
Traynor, J. and Hasnip, J. (1984) 'Sometimes She Makes Me Want to Hit Her', *Community Care*, No. 523, 20–21.
Ungerson, C. (1987) *Policy is Personal: Sex Gender and Informal Care*, London, Tavistock.
Victor, C. (1987) *Old Age in Modern Society*, London, Croom Helm.
Wagner, G. (Chairperson) (1988) *Residential Care: A Positive Choice*, London, HMSO.
Waldrond-Skinner, S. (1976) *Family Therapy: The Treatment of Natural Systems*, London and Boston, Routledge & Kegan Paul.
Walker, A. (1966) 'Pensions and the Production of Poverty in Old Age', in Phillipson, C. and Walker, A. (eds), op. cit.
Wasser, E. (1966) *Creative Approaches in Casework with the Aging*, New York, Family Service Association of America.
Wasser, E. (1971) 'Protective Practice in Serving the Mentally Impaired Aged', *Social Casework*, 52, 8, 510–22.
Weaver, T., Willcocks, D. and Kellaher, L. (1985) *The Business of Care: A Study of Private Residential Homes for Old People*, London, Centre for Environmental and Social Studies in Ageing.
Wenger, G. C. (1984) *The Supportive Network – Coping with Old Age*, London, George Allen & Unwin.
Wheeler, R. (1986) 'Housing Policy and Elderly People', in Phillipson, C. and Walker, A. (eds), op. cit.
Whitehorn, K. (1987) 'Budget Now: No Burden Later', London, *Observer*, 24.5.87.

Whittaker, J. and Garbarino, J. (1983) *Social Support Networks*, New York, Aldine.

Whittaker, J. (1986) 'Integrating Formal and Informal Social Care', *British Journal of Social Work*, 16, Supplement.

Willcocks, D. (1986) 'Residential Care', in Phillipson, C. and Walker, A. (eds), op. cit.

Wilson, J. (1987) 'Helping Groups to Grow', *Community Care*, no. 667, 20–1.

Wilson, K. and James, A. (1987) 'An ultra sensitive area – marital problems', *Community Care*, no. 648, 22–3.

Wright, F. (1986) *Left to Care Alone*, London, Gower.

Index

140   *Index*